EURO 2000™

The Official Book

UEFA
EURO
2000

This edition published in 2000 by Carlton Books Limited
20 Mortimer Street, London W1N 7RD
1 3 5 7 9 10 8 6 4 2
Text and design copyright © 2000 Carlton Books Limited
©The EURO 2000™ Emblem, the Official Mascot and the UEFA European Football Championship™ Trophy are copyrights and trademarks of UEFA.
©L'Emblème de l'EURO 2000™, la Mascotte Officielle et le Trophée du Championnat d'Europe de Football de l'UEFA sont des droits réservés de l'UEFA.
© Het EURO 2000™ Embleem, de Officiële Mascotte en de UEFA European Football Championship™ Beker zijn handelsmerken van de UEFA en genieten levens auteursrechtelijke bescheming.
Manufactured under licence by
Produit fabriqué sous licence officielle par
Onder licentie vervaardigd door
Carlton Books

Project Editor: Vanessa Daubney; Project Art Direction: Brian Flynn; Production: Sarah Corteel; Picture Research: Catherine Costelloe

Printed and bound in Italy

EURO 2000™
The Official Book

UEFA
EURO
2000

KEIR RADNEDGE

CARLTON
BOOKS

Contents

Official Partners of EURO 2000™

Official Suppliers of EURO 2000™

Introduction

In EURO 2000™, the greatest footballing nations of Europe meet over three weeks to contest the coveted Henri Delaunay Trophy. It is a recipe for a football feast served up by some of the finest players in the world. The number of countries competing is whittled down to 16 through qualifying competition and thus includes none of the lower-order nations whose erratic qualities compromise the overall standard of the senior event. UEFA should be proud of the strides its "baby" has taken since its launch in the late 1950s.

Reigning champions: can Germany repeat their Euro 96 triumph without the likes of Jurgen Klinsman?

The progress of the UEFA European Football Championship™ has mirrored that of European football itself. Entry levels have doubled and none of the great nations who stayed aloof from the first tournament, such as old rivals England and Germany, would ever dream of doing so now.

EURO 2000™ is the first major football finals to be co-hosted and the event will be viewed with enormous interest, not least by observers from the governments and national federations of Japan and South Korea, the two countries co-hosting the 2002 FIFA World Cup. EURO 2000™ bosses Alain Courtois from Belgium and Harry Been from Holland agree it has been hard work, but at least they share a common border, a language and an international currency (the euro) and have many cultural and administrative similarities. How well the tournament runs will set the standard for other smaller European nations that dream of co-hosting major events.

Ultimately, of course, EURO 2000™ will be remembered not for the logistics but for the football. If it is as dramatic as the expanded 16-nation finals in England four years ago, football could not kick off the new century in better form.

A clutch of coaches: which of Europe's top national coaches will emerge victorious in EURO 2000™?

The Draw

The drama of EURO 2000™ started with the draw on 12 December 1999 in Brussels – old rivals Germany and England were paired in the same group.

The nations had been seeded with the aim of keeping the top countries as far apart as possible in the group stages to ensure exciting quarter-finals. The splitting of countries into four pools was also designed to prevent so-called "Groups of Death" as in the Germany, Italy, Czech Republic and Russia group in Euro 96; Italy, considered strong challengers, slipped out in the first round.

The top bowl consisted of co-hosts Belgium and Holland, plus defending champions Germany and UEFA's highest-ranked team, Spain. The second pot was decided by recent FIFA World Cup and UEFA European Football Championship™ qualifying performances and held Romania, Norway, Sweden and the Czech Republic. The third pot held France, Italy, Portugal and Yugoslavia and the last held the teams who won through via the play-offs – Denmark, Slovenia, Turkey and England.

UEFA invited 10 players who were members of winning UEFA European Football Championship™ teams to take part in the draw – Viktor Ponedelnik (Soviet Union 1960), Luis Suarez (Spain 1964), Giacinto Facchetti (Italy 1968), Franz Beckenbauer (West Germany 1972), Antonin Paneka (Czechoslovakia 1976), Bernd Schuster (West Germany 1980), Michel Platini (France 1984), current Dutch coach Frank Rijkaard (Holland 1988), John Jensen (Denmark 1992) and Thomas Helmer (Germany 1996).

Before the draw, UEFA president Lennart Johansson pointed out, "With these sixteen teams, you could almost put them in any order and it really would not make too much difference."

Those countries drawn in group D would certainly agree that the seeding has not been a help to the so-called top teams. The general consensus is that this is the hardest group. It consists of co-hosts Holland, the Czech Republic – last time's runners-up and one of the form teams – FIFA World Cup-holders France and 1992 winners Denmark.

The section which drew gasps from the audience of officials, coaches and media was Group A – Germany and England paired in the same group for the second time in five days, following the 2002 FIFA World Cup qualifying draw. They are joined by Romania, who beat England in the group stages of the last FIFA World Cup, and Portugal.

Group C includes another repeat pairing from the FIFA World Cup qualifying draw in neighbours Yugoslavia and Slovenia. They are joined by the highest-ranked team of the 16, Spain, and impressive qualifiers Norway, who won eight out of their 10 games to reach the finals.

Italy are the glamour side in Group B, which also includes co-hosts Belgium as well as 1992 hosts Sweden plus Turkey, who will be aiming to improve on their Euro 96 performance when they lost every game and were the only team not to score a single goal.

The sharpest reaction to the draw came when England were drawn alongside Germany. The history of clashes between these nations adds extra spice to a situation in which both managers have something to prove to their critics. England manager Kevin Keegan, who played in Germany for Hamburg and knows the language well, said, "I won't do handstands and say it's fantastic but it's not the hardest group."

German coach Erich Ribbeck was looking forward to the challenge, saying, "Many times it's better to play against what are considered stronger teams because it inspires better concentration among our own team."

England start the group as clear underdogs, having qualified through the play-offs while Germany and Romania both won their groups, Romania without losing, and Portugal qualified as having the best record of the nine runners-up.

Holland are considered favourites by many, but Dutch coach Frank Rijkaard knows their group is tough. He described recent drawn games with Denmark and the Czech Republic as "difficult and awkward". Holland's match with France is the last game of the group and could decide the section winners.

In the opening game of the championship, Belgium take on Sweden in the King Baudouin (formerly Heysel) Stadium in Brussels. Belgium beat Italy 3–1 in Lecce in a friendly last November and Italy coach Dino Zoff knows they cannot be underestimated. He says, "From what I have seen they are an excellent team." Turkish manager Mustafa Denizli was confident after the draw, saying, "We have been paired with teams that we know and who are no strangers to us. We can make it to the next round. We have a team that can achieve that."

Spain are clear favourites in their group, and coach José Camacho is confident, promising, "There is no reason to be happy or unhappy at the group we have landed in. We will fight hard to ensure we finish on top."

At the end of the first round, of course, only four coaches will have made that dream come true. After that it's knock-out quarter-finals, semi-finals and the final itself in the Feyenoord Stadium in Rotterdam.

Sounds simple – the draw suggests it could be great.

Dutch master: Frank Rijkaard in his playing days.

The Venues

The stadia that will welcome the rest of Europe are a blend of the old and the new. They all meet UEFA's strict demands for both security and spectator comfort, and that means all-seater venues, at least two-thirds covered.

The Amsterdam ArenA and the Arnhem Gelredome have sliding roofs. The Gelredome also has a revolutionary retractable pitch and full air-conditioning. The Gelredome, the Communal du Pays de Charleroi (formerly the Mambourg), and the Jan Breydal in Brussels have had their capacities enlarged to 30,000. The Sclessin Stadium, Liège, was built in what has been described as an English style, with the fans much closer to the pitch than at many European grounds.

The UEFA stadium committee has awarded two of the grounds its prestigious five-star status (Amsterdam ArenA and Feyenoord's De Kuip, Rotterdam), while both the King Baudouin (formerly Heysel, Brussels) and the Philips Stadium (Eindhoven) have four stars.

The Amsterdam ArenA, King Baudouin and De Kuip have all been used many times for international matches as well as UEFA finals, but football is not the only sport to be seen at the EURO 2000™ grounds. The King Baudouin, in particular, has hosted the annual Ivo Van Damme and other athletics competitions, boxing events and the arrival of the Tour de France. Also ArenA, the Gelredome and the Philips Stadium have played host to concerts from the Backstreet Boys to Ray Charles.

The Stadia

Amsterdam ArenA, Amsterdam

Home team: Ajax
Built: 1996
Capacity: 50,000
Address: Arenboulevard 1,
1101 AX Amsterdam Z.O.

- opened 14 August 1996
- sliding roof can be opened or closed in 30 minutes
- floodlighting placed on both sides of the roof so no lighting masts interfere with sight lines
- as well as Ajax, the Dutch national team and the Amsterdam Admirals play here
- hosted the 1998 UEFA Champions League final in which Real Madrid beat Juventus 1–0
- used for concerts by Michael Jackson, Tina Turner and the Rolling Stones

Gelredome, Arnhem

Home team: Vitesse Arnhem
Built: 1998
Capacity: 30,000
Address: Batavierenweg 25, 6841 HN Arnhem

- opened 15 March 1998
- sliding roof, retractable playing field, walkway, air-conditioning system
- has played host to Spice Girls, Backstreet Boys and Janet Jackson concerts
- capacity of 26,000 being increased to 30,000 for EURO 2000™

Jan Breydel Stadium, Bruges

Home teams: Clube Brugge and Cercle Brugge
Built: 1975
Capacity: 30,000
Address: Olympialaan 74, 8200 Bruges

- used by both the town's clubs
- renovated to double capacity for EURO 2000™, mostly behind goals, making it suitable also for cultural events
- former Olympic Stadium
- free access at all four corners for better security

King Baudouin Stadium, Brussels

Home team: Belgian national team
Built: 1930
Capacity: 50,000
Address: Marathonlaan 135, 1020 Brussels

- hosts the opening game of EURO 2000™
- built to commemorate Belgium's centenary
- hosts Belgian internationals, European Champions League and Cup-Winners' Cup finals, Belgian Cup finals, boxing, arrival of the Tour de France, athletics (including the annual Ivo Van Damme Memorial meeting)
- previously known as the Heysel Stadium
- redeveloped and reopened in 1995 with Belgium v. Germany
- only the façade remains from the original design
- largest stadium in Belgium
- hosted its first concert, with Celine Dion, in June 1997

Stade Communal du Pays de Charleroi, Charleroi

Home team: R. Charleroi SC
Built: 1939
Capacity: 30,000
Address: Boulevard Zoe Drion 19, 6000 Charleroi

- formerly known as the Mambourg
- has been gradually redeveloped
- in 1939 Sporting Charleroi built it as their home ground; in 1987 executive boxes were added; in 1992 terracing was replaced by seats

Philips Stadium, Eindhoven

Home team: PSV Eindhoven
Built: 1913
Capacity: 30,000
Address: Frederiklaan 10a, 5616 NH Eindhoven

- one of most modern stadia in Holland
- renovation has been ongoing since 1988
- the ground meets the most up-to-date requirements, with plans under way to cover the corners of the stadium
- the Philips corporation's involvement has ensured one of the finest floodlighting systems anywhere in Europe
- has staged Ray Charles and Eros Ramazzotti concerts

Sclessin Stadium, Liège

Home team: Standard Liège
Built: 1984
Capacity: 30,000
Address: Rue de la Centrale 2, 4000 Liège, Belgium

- considered an English-style stadium with stands close to the pitch
- renovated in three phases, with executive boxes the latest major addition
- one stand was specially designed to allow construction vehicles to enter the stadium whenever needed

Feyenoord Stadium (De Kuip), Rotterdam

Home team: Feyenoord
Built: 1937
Capacity: 50,000
Address: Van Zandvlietplein 1, 3077 AA Rotterdam

- has hosted eight UEFA club finals
- most recent European final was the 1997 Cup-Winners' Cup final in which Barcelona beat Paris Saint-Germain 1–0
- large-scale renovation took place in 1994
- a moat has been dug around the pitch to replace security fences
- the roof extends over 80 per cent of the spectators
- there is an interactive museum

The finals
– match dates, times and venues

All times here GMT (add one hour for BST)

Group A
GERMANY, ROMANIA, PORTUGAL, ENGLAND

12 June
- [ ][ ] Germany v. Romania (Liège 1600)
- [ ][ ] Portugal v. England (Eindhoven 1845)

17 June
- [ ][ ] Romania v. Portugal (Arnhem 1600)
- [ ][ ] England v. Germany (Charleroi 1845)

20 June
- [ ][ ] England v. Romania (Charleroi 1845)
- [ ][ ] Germany v. Portugal (Rotterdam 1845)

Group B
BELGIUM, SWEDEN, TURKEY, ITALY

10 June
- [ ][ ] Belgium v. Sweden (Brussels 1845)

11 June
- [ ][ ] Turkey v. Italy (Arnhem 1230)

14 June
- [ ][ ] Belgium v. Italy (Brussels 1845)

15 June
- [ ][ ] Sweden v. Turkey (Eindhoven 1845)

19 June
- [ ][ ] Belgium v. Turkey (Brussels 1845)
- [ ][ ] Italy v. Sweden (Eindhoven 1845)

Quarter-finals

24 June
Amsterdam 1600
1st Group A v. 2nd Group B (E)

[ ] v. [ ]

24 June
Brussels 1845
1st Group B v. 2nd Group A (F)

[ ] v. [ ]

Semi-finals

28 June
Brussels 1845
E v. H

[ ] v. [ ]

29 June
Amsterdam 1845
F v. G

[ ] v. [ ]

Group C

SPAIN, NORWAY, YUGOSLAVIA, SLOVENIA

13 June

☐☐ Spain v. Norway (Rotterdam 1600)

☐☐ Yugoslavia v. Slovenia (Charleroi 1845)

18 June

☐☐ Spain v. Slovenia (Amsterdam 1600)

☐☐ Norway v. Yugoslavia (Liège 1845)

21 June

☐☐ Yugoslavia v. Spain (Bruges 1600)

☐☐ Slovenia v. Norway (Arnhem 1600)

Group D

HOLLAND, CZECH REPUBLIC, FRANCE, DENMARK

11 June

☐☐ France v. Denmark (Bruges 1600)

☐☐ Holland v. Czech Republic (Amsterdam 1845)

16 June

☐☐ Czech Republic v. France (Bruges 1600)

☐☐ Holland v. Denmark (Rotterdam 1845)

21 June

☐☐ Denmark v. Czech Republic (Liège 1845)

☐☐ France v. Holland (Amsterdam 1845)

25 June

Rotterdam 1600

1st Group D v. 2nd Group C (G)

☐☐☐ v. ☐☐☐

25 June

Bruges 1045

1st Group C v. 2nd Group D (H)

☐☐☐ v. ☐☐☐

Final

2 July

Rotterdam 1800

☐☐☐ v. ☐☐☐

NOTE: THERE IS NO THIRD-PLACE PLAY-OFF

The Qualifying Competition

		P	W	D	L	F	A	Pts
Group 1	ITALY	8	4	3	1	13	5	15
	Denmark	8	4	2	2	11	8	14
	Switzerland	8	4	2	2	9	5	14
	Wales	8	3	0	5	7	16	9
	Belarus	8	0	3	5	4	10	3
Group 2	NORWAY	10	8	1	1	21	9	25
	Slovenia	10	5	2	3	12	14	17
	Greece	10	4	3	3	13	8	15
	Latvia	10	3	4	3	13	12	13
	Albania	10	1	4	5	8	14	7
	Georgia	10	1	2	7	8	18	5
Group 3	GERMANY	8	6	1	1	20	4	19
	Turkey	8	5	2	1	15	6	17
	Finland	8	3	1	4	13	13	10
	Northern Ireland	8	1	2	5	4	19	5
	Moldova	8	0	4	4	7	17	4
Group 4	FRANCE	10	6	3	1	17	10	21
	Ukraine	10	5	5	0	14	4	20
	Russia	10	6	1	3	22	12	19
	Iceland	10	4	3	3	12	7	15
	Armenia	10	2	2	6	8	15	8
	Andorra	10	0	0	10	3	28	0
Group 5	SWEDEN	8	7	1	0	10	1	22
	England	8	3	4	1	14	4	13
	Poland	8	4	1	3	12	8	13
	Bulgaria	8	2	2	4	6	8	8
	Luxembourg	8	0	0	8	2	23	0

		P	W	D	L	F	A	Pts
Group 6	**SPAIN**	8	7	0	1	42	5	21
	Israel	8	4	1	3	25	9	13
	Austria	8	4	1	3	19	20	13
	Cyprus	8	4	0	4	12	21	12
	San Marino	8	0	0	8	1	44	0
Group 7	**ROMANIA**	10	7	3	0	25	3	24
	Portugal	10	7	2	1	32	4	23
	Slovakia	10	5	2	3	12	9	17
	Hungary	10	3	3	4	14	10	12
	Azerbaijan	10	1	1	8	6	26	4
	Liechtenstein	10	1	1	8	2	39	4
Group 8	**YUGOSLAVIA**	8	5	2	1	18	8	17
	Rep Ireland	8	5	1	2	14	6	16
	Croatia	8	4	3	1	13	9	15
	FYR Macedonia	8	2	2	4	13	14	8
	Malta	8	0	0	8	6	27	0
Group 9	**CZECH REPUBLIC**	10	10	0	0	26	5	30
	Scotland	10	5	3	2	15	10	18
	Estonia	10	3	2	5	15	17	11
	Bosnia-Herzegovina	10	3	2	5	14	17	11
	Lithuania	10	3	2	5	8	16	11
	Faroe Islands	10	0	3	7	4	17	3

Play-offs

England bt Scotland 2–0, 0–1   (2–1 on aggregate)

Turkey bt Rep Ireland 1–1, 0–0   (on away goal, 1–1 aggregate)

Denmark bt Israel 5–0, 3–0   (8–0 on aggregate)

Slovenia bt Ukraine 2–1, 1–1   (3–2 on aggregate)

Belgium

Robert Waseige was a few days short of his 60th birthday, thinking more about winding down his career than stepping it up, when he was handed the toughest task in Belgian football.

The national team, the so-called Red Devils, were suffering a depressing lack of hellfire spirit, having won only twice in 11 games. They had lost at home to the Czech Republic, Bulgaria, Egypt and Finland. Georges Leekens, the coach who had taken Belgium to the FIFA World Cup finals in France in 1998, was short of credibility with both public and players.

The Belgian federation turned to veteran coach Waseige who had just completed a stint with Charleroi. As technical committee chairman Karel Vertongen said,

Goal standard: Belgium striker Gilles de Bilde.

"He has all the right qualities. He has experience, wisdom, knowledge of the players – and he is available."

Immediately, a new spirit of optimism invaded Belgian football. Playing hosts – even co-hosts as Belgium and Holland are for EURO 2000™ – presents enormous advantages to any team in a major tournament and Belgium certainly have the pedigree. Top clubs Anderlecht and Brugge have long been powerful contenders in European competition while the national team were UEFA European Football Championship™ runners-up in 1980 and semi-finalists in 1972, to say nothing of FIFA World Cup semi-finalists in 1986.

Immediate results reflected that new spirit. While the qualifying rounds for EURO 2000™ were taking place, Belgium drew 5–5 in a sensational match against Holland, thrashed Morocco 4–0, lost only narrowly by 2–1 away to England and scored a surprise 3–1 victory away to Italy who will be among their first-round rivals in the finals.

COACH

Robert Waseige

Born: August 26, 1939
Appointed: August 1999
Career: Veteran coach who was appointed in an emergency this past summer in succession to Georges Leekens who had guided Belgium to the 1998 FIFA World Cup finals. Waseige played for Liègeois, Racing White and Winterslag – with whom he then began coaching. Earned enormous respect within the Belgium game for the manner in which he achieved success on sometimes thin resources at not only Winterslag but Standard Liège, Lokeren, back at Liègeois and Charleroi. He also had a spell in Portugal with Sporting of Lisbon. Voted Belgian Manager of the Year in 1986, 1994 and 1995.

Striking for goal: Mbo Mpenza (left) escapes Paolo Vanoli in Belgium's shock 3–1 win over Italy last November.

The surprise is that Waseige has not rung major changes in personnel. Key man in midfield remains the long-striding Marc Wilmots from German club Schalke, aided and abetted by Parma's Johan Walem and home-based Yves Vanderhaeghe from Excelsior Mouscron. In attack, Waseige has welcomed aboard Croatia-born striker Branko Strupar to step up the performance pressures on the Mpenza brothers, domestic league top-scorer Toni Brogno and Sheffield Wednesday's Gilles De Bilde.

Waseige will also hope that PSV Eindhoven's Luc Nilis, Belgium's most consistent striker, has second thoughts about his national team retirement.

Whether Belgium's defence can match the attack for talent and discipline is another matter. Ronny Gaspercic, Geert De Vlieger, Filip Dewilde and Philippe Van de Walle all played in goal last season. None of them looked like becoming Michel Preud-homme's successor. That places heavy extra responsibility on the organizational talents of Anderlecht's Lorenzo Staelens at the heart of the defence and on whoever may be called up to support him from a foreign-based cast list which includes Regis Genaux, Bob Peeters and Nico Van Kerckhoven, a team-mate of Wilmots' at Schalke.

Wilmots is worried that Belgian fans may expect too much of their heroes come June. He says, "We deserved to beat Italy but we have to remember to keep our feet on the ground. Italy will not play as disappointingly against us in the finals. At least that result did one good thing – it made the rest of Europe take notice. They will treat us with more respect when they come here for the finals."

European Championship Record

1960: Did not enter	**1980**: Second
1964: Did not qualify	**1984**: First round
1968: Did not qualify	**1988**: Did not qualify
1972: Third	**1992**: Did not qualify
1976: Did not qualify	**1996**: Did not qualify

Czech Republic

The Czech Republic approach EURO 2000™ with the theme "it's now or never" ringing in their ears. Four years ago the Czechs surprised the rest of Europe by finishing as runners-up. The current generation of players has this one last chance to make their talent tell.

Hero status: Karel Poborsky was a key man in 1996.

However, coach Josef Chovanec knows he will need all his players at their best if the 1976 European champions and 1996 runners-up are even to progress from a tough first-round group which pits them against co-hosts and favourites Holland, World Champions France and 1992 winners Denmark. As he says, "We knew it would be tough. There are no weak teams at this level."

The Czechs will take confidence from their remarkable qualifying campaign in which they won all 10 of their matches in a group featuring Scotland, Bosnia-Herzegovina, Lithuania, Estonia and the Faroe Islands. The closest Chovanec's men came to a scare was against Scotland in Prague when the visitors took a 2–0 lead before the Czechs rallied to win 3–2 thanks to a late strike from Jan Koller. Thus the Czechs subsequently made certain of their place in the finals long before anyone else bar Belgium and Holland.

That excellent international sequence lifted the Czechs

COACH

Josef Chovanec

Born: 7 March 1960
Appointed: July 1998
Career: Chovanec was an international midfielder who starred for the former Czechoslovakia at the 1990 FIFA World Cup when they reached the quarter-finals. He had an outstanding playing career with Cheb, Sparta Prague, PSV Eindhoven (Holland) and Sparta again, winning nine league titles and 11 domestic cups during his career in Czechoslovakia and Holland. He was appointed Sparta coach midway through the 1996–97 season, guiding them to the league championship in 1997 and 1998. He succeeded Dusan Uhrin as national coach in summer 1998.

Home comfort: Jan Koller (left) has risen to stardom in Belgian football.

up to second place in the world rankings ahead of FIFA World Cup holders France and behind only Brazil. However, it also brought its own pressures. Few Czech fans will now be happy with anything less than outright victory.

Sweeper Jan Suchoparek and wing-back Tomas Repka – who missed Euro 96 through suspension – are solid in defence while Chovanec's squad boasts a wealth of creative and attacking talent. The emergence of late developer Vladimir Smicer has added power to a midfield already packed with Euro 96 stars including fleet-footed Karel Poborsky, Liverpool's long-striding Patrik Berger and Lazio playmaker Pavel Nedved.

Up front, Chovanec can rely for goals on imposing strikers Jan Koller and Vratislav Lokvenc. Koller will feel at home in the finals because he plays his club football for Belgian outfit Anderlecht. Only five years ago Koller was playing semi-professional football in the Czech fourth division but he has made such rapid progress that he contributed six goals in the European qualifiers and could be one of the stars of the finals.

Chovanec, who succeeded Euro 96 boss Dusan Uhrin, knows all about the big occasion. He played

European Championship Record

1960: Third*	**1980**: Third*
1964: Did not qualify*	**1984**: Did not qualify*
1968: Did not qualify*	**1988**: Did not qualify*
1972: Did not qualify*	**1992**: Did not qualify
1976: Winners*	**1996**: Second

As Czechoslovakia

52 matches for the former Czechoslovakia and was playmaker when they reached the quarter-finals of the 1990 FIFA World Cup in Italy. His performances in that competition helped earn a transfer to PSV Eindhoven so he, like Koller, will relish the opportunity to demonstrate to his old friends exactly what he has achieved.

Another veteran had the last word after the draw, however. Antonin Panenka, who converted the cheeky penalty which beat West Germany in the shoot-out at the 1976 final, said, "This team of ours is close to its best with several players at the peak of their careers. It's too good a chance to miss."

France

France, managed by Roger Lemerre and inspired in attack by Zinedine Zidane, will emulate West Germany if they win the UEFA European Football Championship™. The Germans are the only nation to have held European and world crowns simultaneously, which they did in 1974.

FIFA World Cup-winning pedigree: goalkeeper Fabien Barthez.

But no FIFA World Cup-holding nation has ever gone into the following UEFA European Football Championship™ and underlined their right to rule. When Franz Beckenbauer's West Germans were at their peak, they used the European title success of 1972 as a springboard to FIFA World Cup triumph in 1974. Lemerre, Zidane and co. intend to do it the other way round.

They are not finding the challenge an easy one. If anything, opponents give France a tougher game than ever before out of determination to take the world champions down a peg. The French came into the final weekend of the qualifying competition uncertain whether they would still be in the event at the end of the night.

Results went their way. While Ukraine forced a shock 1–1 draw away to Russia – who had thought they were virtually home and dry – France defeated Iceland 3–2 to find themselves, almost to their own surprise, winners of the group. Iceland gave the French a fright, battling to get back on terms after having been 2–0 down. Then Monaco striker David Trezeguet snapped up a 71st-minute chance and the FIFA World Cup holders were through.

The rest of the world will not, however, see a carbon copy of the side who thrashed Brazil 3–0 in the FIFA World Cup final in July 1998. For one thing, France have a new coach. Aimé Jacquet stepped down after the FIFA World Cup win, handing over the baton to his comparatively unknown assistant Lemerre.

Injuries did not serve Lemerre well in the EURO 2000™ qualifying tournament. Zidane struggled through much of the post-FIFA World Cup season, worn down by a collection of knee injuries and fatigue. Goalkeeper Fabien Barthez, one of the most popular of

COACH

Roger Lemerre

Born: 18 June 1941
Appointed: August 1998
Career: Lemerre played eight times times for France and made a remarkable 414 top-division appearances as a central defender with Sedan, Nantes, Nancy and Lens where he wound down his career in 1975. He turned to coaching with Red Star Paris, Lens, Strasbourg, Esperance (Tunisia) and Red Star again. Lemerre joined the French federation coaching staff in 1985, winning the World Military Championship in 1995. He coached Lens in 1996–97 before returning to the FFF in time for the 1998 FIFA World Cup triumph after which he succeeded Aimé Jacquet as national coach.

the FIFA World Cup-winning players, missed several key matches through injury while Laurent Blanc, Didier Deschamps and Marcel Desailly never quite rekindled their World Cup form for the national team.

On top of that, the perennial French attacking problem remained. Jacquet had been fortunate in the FIFA World Cup that individuals such as Zidane, Thierry Henry, Emmanuel Petit and Lilian Thuram found the route to goal at crucial moments. But consistent danger was notable by its absence. Lemerre will hope that one of the old guard of Stephane Guivarc'h, Trezeguet and Lilian Laslandes may translate domestic club form into the international arena.

France have paid a heavy price for the highly publicized career free fall of Real Madrid striker Nicolas Anelka. When he scored both goals in France's friendly win over England at Wembley in spring 1999, it seemed that the last piece had fallen into place for Lemerre. Instead, after all the furore surrounding his move to Madrid from Arsenal, it will be a major surprise if Anelka, for all his talent, even makes the French squad.

Four years ago, France lost on penalties to the Czech Republic in the European semi-finals. Lacking an in-form striker, they may fear a similar fate overtaking them again.

Sweeping up: veteran French central defender Laurent Blanc.

European Championship Record

1960: Fourth	**1980**: Did not qualify
1964: Did not qualify	**1984**: Winners
1968: Did not qualify	**1988**: Did not qualify
1972: Did not qualify	**1992**: First round
1976: Did not qualify	**1996**: Semi-finalists

Germany

Germany are record European champions, having carried off the Henri Delaunay Trophy in 1972, 1980 and 1996, but the holders are far from up among the favourites this time. Quite the reverse, talk has been more about crises than crowns.

New wave: Bayern Munich's defensive midfielder Jens Jeremies.

Four years ago, under Berti Vogts, Germany beat the Czech Republic at Wembley thanks to a golden goal from Oliver Bierhoff. Then Bierhoff was a substitute, now he is national captain, which illustrates the turnover with which coach Erich Ribbeck has had to cope.

Ribbeck, though a managerial veteran, is comparatively new to this job. Predecessor Berti Vogts was the managerial hero in 1996 but became a scapegoat after FIFA World Cup quarter-final failure against Croatia in France in 1998. Long-time stalwarts such as striker Jürgen Klinsmann and central defender Jürgen Kohler who had helped form the pillar of the team, stepped aside. Attacking sweeper Matthias Sammer was sidelined with serious knee trouble. It says everything about Germany's lack of emerging talent that Lothar Matthäus, now 38, has remained a key man for so long.

Germany began the qualifying campaign badly with a 1–0 defeat away to Turkey in Bursa but then won six in a row with Bierhoff hitting a hat-trick in a 6–1 win over Moldova in Leverkusen. In the end, the Germans needed only to avoid a home defeat by

European Championship Record

1960: Did not enter	**1980**: Winners
1964: Did not enter	**1984**: First round
1968: Did not qualify	**1988**: Semi-finalists
1972: Winners	**1992**: Second
1976: Second	**1996**: Winners

COACH

Erich Ribbeck

Born: 13 June 1937
Appointed: October 1998
Career: Ribbeck played professionally for Wuppertal and Viktoria Koln but gained far greater fame after launching a successful coaching career with Borussia Münchengladbach, Rot-Weiss Essen, Eintracht Frankfurt, Kaiserslautern, Borussia Dortmund, Bayer Leverkusen and, finally, Bayern Munich. He was persuaded out of retirement by the German federation when Berti Vogts quit in the autumn of 1998.

Standing tall: Mehmet Scholl rides a tackle.

Turkey in Munich's Olympic Stadium to ensure they topped qualifying Group Three. They managed it, but only just.

Adding to German concerns are memories of a humiliating pre-season trip to contest the controversial Confederations Cup in Mexico when a 4–0 defeat by Brazil was exacerbated by a 2–0 upset at the hands of the United States. "How could Germany embarrass themselves like that?" and "The world is laughing at German soccer now" were just two of the headlines.

Vogts thought those defeats merely underlined his long-time concerns at a lack of quality within the Bundesliga being enhanced by the clubs signing cheaper foreign players in preference to developing their own talent. As Vogts said, "The motor won't start if there's no fuel in the tank."

However, Germany will not be short of determination to make the most of what talents they do possess. They are fortunate, for example, to boast two outstanding goalkeepers. Oliver Kahn has developed by leaps and bounds under the coaching tutelage of old favourite Sepp Maier with both Bayern and the national team while Borussia Dortmund's Jens Lehmann would walk into any other national team. Lehmann demonstrated his talents with no fewer than three superb penalty saves in Dortmund's UEFA Cup third-round win over Rangers.

In defence, Ribbeck has experimented with a four-man back line instead of the now traditional German three-man system. Matthäus remains a key man, however, with Bayern team-mate Jens Jeremies, one of

the European game's most aggressive defensive midfielders, a likely successor.

In attack, it all depends on Bierhoff, scorer of both goals in Germany's 2–1 win over the Czech Republic in the 1996 final. He has a lot of responsibility, needing to make up with his goals for shortcomings elsewhere.

 # The Netherlands

Frank Rijkaard knows all about UEFA European Football Championship™ glory. Holland's national coach was a pivotal member of the Dutch side who beat the Soviet Union 2–0 in the 1988 final in Munich. Now he has the opportunity to make history – no European title-winning player has ever graduated to managing the champions.

Defensive anchor: Frank De Boer is a cornerstone for both the Dutch national team and Spanish club Barcelona.

Holland were placed in a tough group by the draw, along with FIFA World Cup-holders France and former European champions Denmark and the Czech Republic. But the Dutch all-stars will not be intimidated. Whatever their failings down the years, a lack of confidence in their ability has never been a factor.

One problem for Holland is the fans' tendency to compare present-day stars with the total football side of the early 1970s when Johan Cruyff's inspiration lifted Ajax to three successive European Cup victories and the

Dutch national team to the 1974 FIFA World Cup final. Observers said that this was a one-off generation of great players but a decade later Holland gloried in the Euro-winning achievements of Ruud Gullit, Marco Van Basten and Rijkaard. The present generation cannot be far behind in terms of talent.

De Boer twins Frank in the centre of defence and Ronald in midfield, wingers Boudewijn Zenden and Marc Overmars, midfield tigers Clarence Seedorf and Edgar Davids plus strikers Patrick Kluivert and Dennis Bergkamp

COACH

Frank Rijkaard

Born: 30 September 1962
Appointed: August 1998
Career: One of the greatest Dutch footballers of all time, Rijkaard was equally brilliant as a sweeper, orthodox central defender or midfield playmaker. He starred at Ajax for eight years, then, after half a season with Zaragoza, earned greater renown with Milan in the late 1980s and early 1990s. He won the Champions Cup twice with Milan and once against Milan after returning to Ajax. He retired from playing in 1996 and joined the Dutch coaching staff in time for the 1998 FIFA World Cup, after which he was promoted to boss in succession to Real Madrid-bound Guus Hiddink.

Old-fashioned values: Arsenal winger Marc Overmars.

are among the most-coveted superstars in world football. They have won all the major trophies between them with some of Europe's greatest clubs – Barcelona, Ajax, Real Madrid, Juventus – and took Holland to the FIFA World Cup semi-finals in France. There they lost to Brazil on a penalty shoot-out, a painful rerun of their two previous UEFA European Football Championship™ exits at the hands of Denmark in the semi-finals in 1992 and France in the quarter-finals in 1996.

Rijkaard's most pressing need, then, appears to be instilling in his players the confidence to keep their nerve under pressure. History shows that Rijkaard and his team-mates lost their first match in the 1988 finals, against the Soviet Union, but recovered to take ultimate revenge in the final.

As co-hosts, Holland were already certain of their place in the European finals and had no need to fret over the qualifying competition. Instead, they set off on the long, friendly road to EURO 2000™ with a 2–0 win over Peru in Eindhoven in October 1998. It was Rijkaard's last taste of success for a very long time. A 1–1 draw against the Czech Republic in Holland's last match of 1999 – back in Eindhoven – was Rijkaard's 11th consecutive outing without a win.

Cruyff, watching as a television analyst, was bitingly critical of players, many of whom he had coached and educated in the game as teenagers. But most other managers would envy Rijkaard players such as Juventus goalkeeper Edwin Van der Sar, Manchester United centre-back Jaap Stam plus the Arsenal and Barcelona contingents. As Rijkaard says, "Considering the hard

programmes our players have with their clubs, it's logical they find it difficult to apply themselves over two years of friendly matches. But remember, all the time we are building up confidence and team spirit." That, remembering some of the Dutch débâcles of the past, could make all the difference.

European Championship Record

1960: Did not enter	**1980**: First round
1964: Did not qualify	**1984**: Did not qualify
1968: Did not qualify	**1988**: Winners
1972: Did not qualify	**1992**: Semi-finalists
1976: Third	**1996**: Quarter-finalists

Italy

Italy are one of the great underachievers at UEFA European Football Championship™ level. Despite their proud football history, despite the power and wealth of their clubs, despite their status as three-times world champions, the Azzurri have provided their passionate fans with more depression than delight in the continent's pre-eminent national team event.

Security guard: central defender Fabio Cannavaro.

The Italians did win in 1968, but even then they struggled with the weight of expectation in front of their own fans. They defeated the Soviet Union only on the toss of a coin in the semi-finals and needed a replay to defeat Yugoslavia in the final. Italy's goalkeeper then, a man who knows all about the trials and tribulations of life with the Italian national side, was Dino Zoff.

Now Zoff is national coach, having succeeded Cesare Maldini after Italy lost on penalties to hosts France in the quarter-finals of the 1998 FIFA World Cup. All Italy hopes Zoff will prove as talismanic a coach as he was a player when he won an Italian record 112 international caps and captained them to glory in the 1982 FIFA World Cup in Spain.

Italy began promisingly under the new man in the autumn of 1998. They won 2–0 away to Wales and by the same score at home to Switzerland with superstars such as Christian Vieri and Alessandro Del Piero firing on all cylinders. Crucially, goals from Pippo Inzaghi and Antonio Conte earned a 2–1 win away to their most dangerous group rivals, Denmark, in Copenhagen in March 1999.

COACH

Dino Zoff

Born: 28 February 1942
Appointed: August 1998
Career: Zoff took Italy's record for the most international appearances when he kept goal for the Azzurri for the 112th and last time against Sweden in 1983. He won just about every prize with Napoli and Juventus as well as the UEFA European Football Championship™ (1968) and FIFA World Cup (as captain, 1982) with Italy. After retiring from playing, he coached Juventus to UEFA Cup success before moving to Lazio where he rose from coach to general manager and on to president. Zoff returned to management as national coach in succession to Cesare Maldini after the 1998 FIFA World Cup.

Attacking inspiration: Juventus' Alessandro Del Piero is one of the world's finest forwards.

Then the motor began to falter. A home draw against Belarus was a hint of problems to come. Wales were beaten 4–0 and a further point was gained from a goalless draw away to Switzerland. Thus they began the 1999–2000 season needing just one point from their final two group matches. At 2–0 up at home to Denmark, Italy appeared home and dry. But, amazingly, the masters of defence conceded three goals and lost 2–3. They scraped out a goalless draw away to Belarus in their last group match to sneak into the finals.

As if the *tifosi* needed their national team's plight underlined, Italy lost their customary status among the top seeds at the draws for both the 2002 FIFA World Cup Korea/Japan and the finals of EURO 2000™. To compound it all, they lost 3–1 at home to struggling Belgium in a friendly.

Of course, all is not lost while Italy can boast such a wonderful array of talent from which to choose their team. Francesco Toldo and Gianluigi Buffon, the nephew of former international Lorenzo Buffon, are the latest two outstanding products of the *Serie A* goalkeepers production line. In front of them, Zoff can mix and match the experience of his captain, Paolo Maldini, with

the youthful defensive aggression of Fabio Cannavaro – who learned his football as a ballboy watching Diego Maradona at Napoli – and Alessandro Nesta.

Midfield is the sector where Zoff may have the greatest problems despite the playmaking talents of Roma skipper Francesco Totti. By contrast, Italy appear awesome up front where Del Piero will supply the passes for Vieri, who cost Internazionale a world record £31 million from Lazio last summer.

Italy are not short of talent. It's whether Zoff can get the mix right that will determine the success of their campaign, and probably Zoff's job prospects, too.

European Championship Record

1960: Did not enter	**1980**: Fourth
1964: Did not qualify	**1984**: Did not qualify
1968: Winners	**1988**: Semi-finalists
1972: Did not qualify	**1992**: Did not qualify
1976: Did not qualify	**1996**: First round

Norway

Norway have never before appeared in the finals of the UEFA European Football Championship™ but none of their opponents will underestimate a side which reached the second round of the FIFA World Cup in France and won eight of their 10 qualifying matches on the road to Belgium and Holland.

Danger man: Manchester United's Ole Gunnar Solskjaer.

European Championship Record

1960: Did not qualify	**1980**: Did not qualify
1964: Did not qualify	**1984**: Did not qualify
1968: Did not qualify	**1988**: Did not qualify
1972: Did not qualify	**1992**: Did not qualify
1976: Did not qualify	**1996**: Did not qualify

Such an imposing list of results did not appear likely at the beginning of Norway's post-FIFA World Cup era. For one thing, they changed their manager. Egil Olsen, the coach who put Norway on the international map albeit amid some controversy over his pragmatic tactics, decided to call it a day and handed over to Nils Johan Semb. Semb's first match in charge was a goalless friendly against Romania and his second a shock 3–1 home defeat by Latvia at the start of the European qualifying tournament.

A 2–1 win away to Slovenia was followed by a 2–2 draw at home to Albania which provoked the first serious murmurings of discontent among fans and media. They had become used to the taste of qualifying match success and Semb's own qualifications were called into doubt. He had, after all, worked on the federation coaching staff for much of the 1990s rather than out in the club world.

Fortunately, Semb's qualities were appreciated by the players, many of whom had worked under him in the Norwegian youth and Under-21 squads. They responded to his style, and to his difficulties, and the corner was turned in a 2–0 win away to the awkward Greeks in March 1999. Manchester United's Ole Gunnar Solskjaer scored both goals. Georgia were beaten 4–1 away and 1–0 at home and a subsequent 2–1 win away to Albania meant a five-point lead at the top of Group Two.

Now fans and media could see the fruits of Semb's work in bringing the younger players through to refresh the nucleus of Olsen's side. The evidence has been published around the world since Norway's name went into the EURO 2000™ draw boasting a status of seventh

COACH

Nils Johan Semb

Born: 24 February 1959
Appointed: August 1998
Career: Semb played all his part-time professional career with minor Norwegian club Orn Horten between 1976 and 1985. He began coaching with EIK Tonsberg and joined the federation in 1990 as number two to the Olympic squad. He later coached the Under-20s and Under-23s before succeeding the long-serving Egil Olsen after Norway's run to the second round of the 1998 FIFA World Cup.

place in the FIFA world rankings. When they lost 1–0 at home to Germany in a friendly shortly before the draw for the EURO 2000™ finals, it was a first defeat in 15 matches – a proud record for a team once considered to be one of the weakest in Europe. In fact, football historians had to go back to 1934 to find the last time Norway had been unbeaten in a calendar year – and, in 1934, the national side played only four games.

The difference now is not only in the quality of Norway's football but the emergence of a generation of outstanding footballers. Tore Andre Flo may be considered Norway's top striker thanks to his goals for his country and for Chelsea in the English Premiership, but Norway boast an embarrassment of riches when it comes to an attacking partner. Solskjaer was the scorer of Manchester United's dramatic Champions League-winning goal against Bayern Munich in Barcelona last season but he faces tough competition from Tottenham's Steffen Iversen and the new wonderboy of Norwegian football, Rosenborg striker John Carew. Foreign clubs have kept close watch on Carew ever since he began scoring goals regularly for the Under-21 side. A boyhood fan of Liverpool, he could be one of the revelations of the European finals.

Former coach Olsen ensured that all his players accepted a role as a member of the engine room of the team and put in all the hard work necessary. Such discipline has earned most of Norway's key players contracts abroad. Midfield is no exception with bearded Erik Mykland playing in Greece with Panathinaikos and Oyvind Leonhardsen in England with Tottenham. Such a wealth of experience could prove vital in Holland and Belgium.

Action man: Tottenham midfielder Oyvind Leonhardsen.

Portugal

Portugal's footballers have been described as the "Brazilians of Europe". Certainly, the language is the same off the pitch, but on it there is one enormous difference – Brazil score goals with a consistency Portugal can only envy.

Threatening behaviour: striker Joao Pinto.

No matter the identity of the national coach, Portugal play a brand of football that is unique in Europe. Their technical ability is delightful to watch and they weave artistic patterns that leave opposing defenders dizzy; but putting the ball in the net is another matter. That is likely to be Portugal's Achilles heel in Belgium and Holland. Portugal were top scorers in the qualifying tournament with 32 goals in their 10 matches in Group Seven in which they finished runners-up to Romania, but no fewer than 20 of those goals were scored in three matches against Liechtenstein (twice) and Azerbaijan. When it came to close combat with the Romanians, Portugal lost 1–0 at home and managed a 1–1 draw away in Bucharest. That suggests that Portugal have not found a way to cope with the lessons of the 1996 finals when they played the most delicately entertaining football of the event but lost in the quarter-finals on a penalty shoot-out to the Czech Republic.

Portugal will bring much the same team to Belgium and Holland and many of those key men have been playing together for more than a decade, ever since they won the World Youth Cup twice at the end of the 1980s and turn of the 1990s.

In goal is Vitor Baia, once considered to be Europe's finest goalkeeper when Bobby Robson took him along

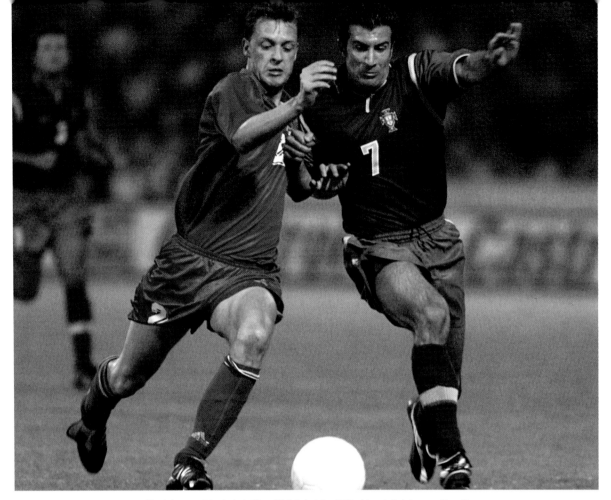

Captain consistent: Luis Figo (right) holds off Liechtenstein's Jurgen Ospelt.

from FC Porto to Barcelona in 1996. Injuries have frayed Baia's talent and he was sent back to Porto on loan this season. At least it gave him a chance to regain fitness and form so that he can defy the rest of Europe come June.

Midfield is the vital area of the pitch for Portugal. This is where the likes of Fiorentina's Manuel Rui Costa and Internazionale's Paulo Sousa knit together the clearances coming out of defence and the knock-backs from the forwards. They are the men who decide whether to attack through the middle where Joao Vleira Pinto lurks, or wide right where Barcelona skipper Luis Figo waits to use his pace and skill.

National coach Humberto Coelho was an outstanding central defender in the 1970s and hopes to harness the players' desire to succeed in what may be their last major international challenge. He says, "Perhaps, for some of our older players, this is going to be their last chance to win a European Championship. We reached the semi-finals in 1984 with a previous generation of players. Now it is the turn of the present generation to rise to the occasion. We accept that

teams like Holland and France will be talked about as favourites and not us. But tournaments are not won by talking, they are won by playing. We are going with the intention of winning and I have total confidence in my team's ability to do just that."

Whatever happens to Portugal in Belgium and Holland, they will return home secure in the knowledge that, next time, they will not have to worry about the qualifying tournament; they will be hosts, thus qualifying directly.

European Championship Record

1960: Did not qualify	**1980**: Did not qualify
1964: Did not qualify	**1984**: Semi-finalists
1968: Did not qualify	**1988**: Did not qualify
1972: Did not qualify	**1992**: Did not qualify
1976: Did not qualify	**1996**: Quarter-finalists

Romania

Gheorghe Hagi has achieved the first part of his mission by leading Romania back to the finals of the UEFA European Football Championship™. That was why he came out of international retirement midway through last year having apparently waved goodbye to the national team after the 1998 FIFA World Cup.

"I could not resist the challenge," says Hagi, "especially when it was coming closer to our matches against Hungary in the qualifying competition."

Hagi might have added that he also has a score to settle with the UEFA European Football Championship™ after Romania were denied a goal in the 1996 finals when a shot from Ioan Lupescu ricocheted out into play from a stanchion in the goal and was not awarded by the referee. "This time," says

European Championship Record	
1960: Did not qualify	**1980**: Did not qualify
1964: Did not qualify	**1984**: First round
1968: Did not qualify	**1988**: Did not qualify
1972: Did not qualify	**1992**: Did not qualify
1976: Did not qualify	**1996**: First round

Hagi, "we do not intend to allow any such incident to make so much difference for us."

Emerich Jenei is back in charge of Romania now. Jenei coached the Steaua Bucharest side who won the European Champions Cup in 1986, beating Barcelona on penalties in Seville, and was in charge of the national team which lost by the same method in the second round of the FIFA World Cup finals in 1990. Luck has not smiled on the Romanians since then. They were eliminated from the 1994 FIFA World Cup quarter-finals on penalties by Sweden, suffered their "ghost goal" upset at Euro 96 and lost narrowly to a real penalty against Croatia, converted by Davor Suker, in the second round in France 98.

Jenei believes Romania are long overdue a change of fortune. He says, "Our players are experienced enough to go all the way in pursuit of the championship. They have been together, most of them, for many years. It is right that they should want to climax so many successful years with a great performance and a great achievement. All we have lacked until now has been a little self-confidence. It's a national characteristic

Hat-trick hero: Romania striker Adrian Ilie.

Experience and ambition: Romania's mixture of veterans and new boys intend to make up for bad luck and lost time.

that I am trying to coach out of them."

Victor Piturca, who was replaced controversially as manager after the qualifying competition, had just been installed as national coach when Romania opened their qualifying account with a 7–0 thrashing of

COACH

Emerich Jenei

Born: 28 March 1937
Appointed: November 1999
Career: The most respected coach in Romanian football history, Jenei guided army club Steaua Bucharest to their historic European Champions Cup victory over Barcelona in 1986 – the first eastern European side to win the top club prize. Later, he took the national team to the second round of the 1990 FIFA World Cup. Jenei moved abroad and was briefly national coach of Hungary, but he returned in late 1999 after the controversial sacking of Victor Piturca following a power struggle with Romania's senior players.

Liechtenstein. Veteran central defender Gica Popescu scored the first goal and Valencia's star striker Adrian Ilie contributed a hat-trick to justify his reputation as one of the most dangerous forwards in Europe.

A 1–0 victory away to Portugal – clearly the Romanians' most dangerous rivals – brought enormous psychological encouragement and rekindled confidence in a manner which proved infectious. Before the first of the two matches against old neighbours and rivals Hungary, playmaker Hagi succumbed to pressure to reconsider. He duly masterminded a dominant first-half performance that brought decisive goals for Ilie and Dorinul Munteanu and, ultimately, a 2–0 win.

Now Hagi, who plays his club football for the Turkish giants Galatasaray, shares Jenei's confidence about the trip to Belgium and Holland, saying, "We have a lot of players who have been in the squad for ten years. Why shouldn't we think of ending our careers in glory?"

Spain

Any national team who bring a strike partnership comparable to Fernando Morientes and Raul to the finals of a major tournament should be considered a threat. But Spain as a team have established a reputation for never adding up to the sum of the individual parts.

World Cup survivor: Bilbao forward Julen Guerrero.

European Championship Record

1960: Did not qualify	**1980**: First round
1964: Winners	**1984**: Second
1968: Did not qualify	**1988**: First round
1972: Did not qualify	**1992**: Did not qualify
1976: Did not qualify	**1996**: Quarter-finalists

As befits a country which boasts clubs such as Real Madrid, Barcelona and Athletic Bilbao, the Spanish are regular contenders for the major prizes, but too often they fail to come up with the goods – just as they failed at the 1998 FIFA World Cup, eliminated in the first round.

Long-serving Basque coach Javier Clemente survived that footballing disaster but a subsequent 3–2 defeat by Cyprus was the last straw. Out went Clemente and in came José Camacho, the former Real Madrid defender who had been a stalwart of the Spanish team in the 1982 FIFA World Cup, which Spain hosted.

Camacho immediately set about giving the national team a more positive look and feel. Under Clemente, the national squad had remained comparatively unchanged with the coach relying on the same players whether they were first choice with their clubs or not. Camacho went for form players and was rewarded with a high-scoring performance that earned Spain a place among the top seeds when the EURO 2000™ draw was made.

Spain won all their seven qualifying matches under Camacho, a sequence which included 9–0 home thrashings of Austria and San Marino and a 6–0 win away to San Marino minnows. Raul, the Real Madrid forward who is probably Europe's most outstanding young player, scored hat-tricks at home to Austria and away to San Marino while Barcelona's versatile Luis Enrique claimed a treble of his own in the home destruction of San Marino.

Since Raul also finished the season as 25-goal top scorer in the league, with Morientes claiming 19, it is no wonder that Spain were considered a team to avoid at the draw. Equally important to their success in the qualifiers and prospects in the finals is the Barcelona captain Pep Guardiola, one of the few home-grown players established at the Catalan club, and the midfield anchor for both club and country. Guardiola is the first point of call for any pass coming out of defence and Camacho has surrounded him with selfless but skilful assistants such as Gaizka Mendieta of Valencia and Atlético Madrid's Juan Carlos Valeron with Real Madrid's Guti and Barcelona's Xavi in the wings. Ahead of them, Bilbao's experienced Julen Guerrero – a survivor from Spain's 1994 FIFA World Cup outfit – and Joseba Etxeberria extend the variety of talents on offer.

The heart of defence remains the control area of Real Madrid skipper Fernando Hierro, now a tower of strength back in his proper position after a surprisingly goal-strewn period in the middle of his career as an attacking midfielder. Hierro knows what it takes to win European prizes after starring at the heart of the Real Madrid side who beat Juventus to win the UEFA Champions League in 1998.

When Spain found themselves in a finals group featuring unfashionable Norway, Slovenia and Yugoslavia, the media grew more excited than ever over their EURO 2000™ prospects. Camacho would have none of it. As he said, "We were favourites to be hosts in 2004, remember, and look what happened there." What happened was that Spain lost the political battle to outsiders Portugal. Camacho does not want his own European efforts undermined by similar, fatal, complacency.

COACH

José Antonio Camacho

Born: 8 June 1955
Appointed: October 1998
Career: A hard-tackling full-back or stopper, Camacho played all his career with Real Madrid and made a then record 81 appearances for Spain, including the 1982 FIFA World Cup and 1984 UEFA European Football Championship™. He re-emerged as a pragmatic but positive coach with Español (twice) and Seville. Appointed Real Madrid coach in the summer of 1998, he quit after 22 days following a row over his choice of assistants. That left him free to take the national team job after the departure of Javier Clemente in early autumn 1998.

Real power: striker Fernando Morientes of Real Madrid.

Sweden

Tommy Svensson, Sweden's coach when they reached the semi-finals of the 1992 UEFA European Football Championship™ and third place at the subsquent 1994 FIFA World Cup, will be a spectator at EURO 2000™. But Sweden's presence, and whatever success they achieve, may all be traced back to the day he took charge at the start of the 1990s.

Hard to beat: striker Kennet Andersson.

European Championship Record

1960: Did not enter	**1980**: Did not qualify
1964: Did not qualify	**1984**: Did not qualify
1968: Did not qualify	**1988**: Did not qualify
1972: Did not qualify	**1992**: Semi-finalists
1976: Did not qualify	**1996**: Did not qualify

At that time, Sweden were considered a once-great European power in serious decline. Denmark and even Norway had overtaken them as top nation in the Nordic countries, domestic attendances were falling and all the top players left for lucrative contracts in southern Europe just as soon as they could. What

Svensson achieved, as much as results out on the pitch, was to give Swedish football back its pride.

Any observer glancing through the team now managed by Svensson's successor, Tommy Soderberg, may consider it short on star quality, but that is no problem for the Swedes. Their secret of success is teamwork. As Patrick Andersson, key central defender under both Svensson and Soderberg once said, "We concentrate on doing the simple things well. We do not have the players or the style to be too clever. We may not be the prettiest team to watch but we will be one of the hardest to beat."

England found that to their cost in the European qualifiers, losing 2–1 in Sweden and drawing 0–0 at Wembley. The frustration of being outplayed, after a bright early start, in Sweden was too much for England's pride and Paul Ince was sent off after a bad foul on Henrik Larsson. In the end, of course, England had the Swedes to thank for the chance to attend the finals. It was the Swedes' 2–0 win over Poland – a match meaningless to them in points terms – that

Honest endeavour: Sweden topped their qualifying group and gave England a helping hand.

allowed England into the play-offs.

"I always thought the Swedes would do an honest job for us," said England coach Kevin Keegan, and that summed up the Swedish approach. They will not underestimate the challenge ahead of them as outsiders at EURO 2000™ but they will not be fazed by it, either – even in the absence of Celtic forward Larsson, who suffered a severe leg fracture in a UEFA Cup tie against Lyon last October. Soderberg says, "It would be wonderful to have him fit for the finals but normally it takes a player up to nine months to get over such a serious injury. We will not worry. We have Kennet Andersson with all his experience and plenty of other good strikers who can do a job for us."

These include home-based Marcus Allback of Orgryte and exports Jorgen Petterson (Kaiserslautern, Germany) Yksel Osmanovski (Bari, Italy) and Mattias Jonsson (Brondby, Denmark). Midfield is founded around Sunderland's Stefan Schwarz, a veteran of the 1992 and 1994 sides, while security at the back is provided by the rock-line Patrick Andersson, Teddy Lucic and Joachim Bjorklund.

Nations perceived to possess greater soccer personality, such as Spain and Portugal, attracted much of the attention during the qualifying tournament, and the Swedes' achievements went comparatively unnoticed. Yet they dropped only two points in qualifying, beating Poland, Bulgaria and Luxembourg twice as well as winning and drawing against England. Not only that, but they conceded only one goal, the best defensive record in the qualifying competition. Their EURO 2000™ rivals have been warned.

COACH

Tommy Soderberg

Born: 19 August 1948
Appointed: October 1997
Career: Soderberg made his name as a coach with Djurgarden in the mid 1980s, having spent his playing career in the lower leagues. He had guided AIK Stockholm to the 1992 league title when he was appointed on a part-time basis to assist the national team coaching staff. Soderberg went on to become manager of the Under-21s and succeeded Tommy Svensson after the failure to qualify for the 1998 FIFA World Cup finals.

Yugoslavia

Yugoslavia return to action at the UEFA European Football Championship™ finals for the first time since 1984 with the ambition of showing the rest of the continent what they have been missing all this time.

Events far beyond the control of footballers have been mostly to blame. The Slavs failed to qualify for the finals in West Germany in 1988. They qualified in 1992, only to be excluded by UEFA on security grounds two weeks before the tournament in Sweden, after the eruption of fighting in the Balkans.

The ongoing political crisis prevented Yugoslavia even entering the 1996 UEFA European Football Championship™ but they did return to the international mainstream at the 1998 FIFA World Cup, reaching the second round before losing to Holland.

Now they have their date with fate, back in the European finals.

Qualifying was anything but simple, the group fixtures being disrupted by the NATO raids on Serbia and Kosovo. At one stage, it appeared very likely that Yugoslavia's footballers would miss out again because of affairs of state. Enormous controversy arose, for example, when their qualifying visit to the Republic of Ireland had to be postponed after the Irish government refused to issue visas at the last minute.

"These are not our problems, we just want to play a football match," said star forward Predrag Mijatovic, who was one of the Yugoslav export footballers most voceriferous in leading anti-NATO demonstrations in Spain where he was playing for Real Madrid.

In the end, the qualifying programme was revived with the decisive tie – Yugoslavia away to neighbours Croatia in Zagreb – being played on the last matchday. Croatia, third at the 1998 FIFA World Cup, were expected to win narrowly and qualify. Instead their

Back in the frame: Yugoslav forward Dejan Stankovic.

COACH

Vujadin Boskov

Born: 9 May 1931
Appointed: July 1999
Career: Boskov was brought out of retirement to take over from Milan Zivadinovic midway through the European qualifying campaign. Boskov was a fine wing-half with Vojvodina Novisad before ending his playing career in Italy with Sampdoria in 1961. He achieved enormous success coaching Vojvodina, Ajax, Feyenoord, Real Madrid, Gijon and Ascoli before returning to Sampdoria as boss in 1986. Boskov built the finest team in the club's history, winning the Cup-Winners' Cup in 1990 and finishing Champions Cup runners-up in 1992.

Match winner: forward Predrag Mijatovic escapes the Macedonia defence.

nerves got the better of them and Yugoslavia took advantage to force a 2–2 draw. So Yugoslavia go to Belgium and Holland instead. Mijatovic and Dejan Stankovic scored the crucial goals and Yugoslavia hung on to their point despite having to play more than half the match without right-back Zoran Mirkovic, who was sent off just before the interval.

The qualifying success – in which Yugolsavia were helped by the Irish Republic's simultaneous last-match slip-up against FYR Macedonia – was a triumph in particular for veteran coach Vujadin Boskov. He had been brought out of retirement to replace Milan Zividinovic and realized quickly that the team needed reviving with new blood.

This means that veteran stars such as Dragan Stojkovic and Dejan Savicevic might be overlooked when Boskov comes to name his squad for the finals. But, whether he promotes a number of the outstanding Under-21 side or not, Boskov will still rely on many of the seniors who took Yugoslavia to the last FIFA World Cup.

Striker Mijatovic, scorer of Real Madrid's winning goal in the 1998 Champions League final, is one such

European Championship Record

1960: Second	**1984**: First round
1964: Did not qualify	**1988**: Did not qualify
1968: Second	**1992**: Qualified, but
1972: Did not qualify	banned for security
1976: Fourth	reasons
1980: Did not qualify	**1996**: Did not enter

player. He is now with Fiorentina in Italy. Sweeper Sinisa Mihajlovic also plays in Italy, starring for Lazio. Mihajlovic is more than a key defender; he has scored more goals direct from free kicks than any other player in Italian football and will be a danger from virtually any range at EURO 2000™.

As Velibor Vasovic, Champions Cup-winning captain of Ajax Amsterdam in 1971 and now the Slavs' Under-21 boss, says, "We have some of the most talented players, both young and old, in Europe. I believe their time has come."

Denmark

Denmark were shock winners of the UEFA European Football Championship™ when they turned up at a fortnight's notice to win in Sweden in 1992. The rest of Europe immediately learned the lesson – don't underestimate the national team Bo Johansson brings to Belgium and Holland.

Made it! Denmark celebrate their play-off victory over Israel.

Denmark have rebuilt their team several times during the past two decades. In the early 1980s they first secured international headlines in the modern era with a side built around diminutive European Footballer of the Year Allan Simonsen. They reached the FIFA World Cup finals in 1986 with the team which earned them the nickname of "Danish Dynamite" for the explosive manner of their attacking play.

One of the last links with that team was severed when veteran forward Michael Laudrup retired from football after the 1998 FIFA World Cup. An extra handicap for the Danes in the present UEFA European

COACH

Bo Johansson

Born: 27 November 1942
Appointed: July 1996
Career: Swede Johansson took over as boss of the club for whom he was playing, Kalmar, aged 31 in 1973. Subsequently, he coached Lindsvall, Kalmar again, Osters Vaxjo (twice league champions), Panathinaikos (Greece), Iceland's national team, Silkeborg (Denmark) and Helsingborgs (back in Sweden). He succeeded Richard Moller Nielsen as national coach of Denmark.

Football Championship™ is the fact that his younger brother Brian decided to quit the national team after the 3–2 quarter-final defeat by Brazil in Nantes.

Johansson thus had to start largely from scratch when it came to EURO 2000™ and the initial signs were not good. Denmark secured only two points from their first four qualifying matches and when they conceded two goals to Italy's Diego Fuser and Christian Vieri in little more than half an hour in Naples, elimination was staring them in the face. Switzerland appeared favourites to clinch second spot in the group behind Italy.

But one quality which the Danes have never lacked is spirit. In a dramatic second-half comeback, they scored three times in 25 minutes with Jon Dahl Tomasson's winning goal putting the group pressure on Italy. Ultimately, Denmark squeezed into the play-offs because of their better head-to-head record against Switzerland.

Johansson's new side has gradually come together, an effective mixture of youth and experience. The veteran talent is represented by goalkeeper Peter Schmeichel, PSV Eindhoven's left-back Jan Heintze, central defender Jes Hogh of Chelsea and versatile midfielder Thomas Helveg who had been underrated by Danish fans until emerging as a star in Italy's *Serie A* with Udinese and Milan.

As Johansson said, "Over the past twelve months we have been able to build a team around the same eight or nine players. This has provided stability within which we have been able to experiment and develop with tactics and with newer, younger, footballers."

One of the men to make the international breakthrough has been Feyenoord forward Jon Dahl Tomasson who would, naturally, love the opportunity to go back to his "home" stadium in Rotterdam to play in the EURO 2000™ final. Tomasson made his name in Holland originally with Heerenveen, had a depressing time of it in the English Premiership with Newcastle, and regained his enthusiasm, form and eye for goal after joining Feyenoord. Six goals in the last five qualifiers plus three out of the eight fired home in the two-leg play-off triumph over Israel marked Tomasson out as the man to watch when Danish dynamite explodes on EURO 2000™.

Back home: John Dahl Tomasson made his name in Dutch football.

European Championship Record

1960: Did not qualify	**1980**: Did not qualify
1964: Fourth	**1984**: Semi-finalists
1968: Did not qualify	**1988**: First round
1972: Did not qualify	**1992**: Winners
1976: Did not qualify	**1996**: First round

England

England bring a heavy burden to EURO 2000™, the overexpectation fostered by a national passion built on the legend of the home of modern football. Fans and media will never settle for anything less than victory, be it the UEFA European Football Championship™, FIFA World Cup or Champions League.

Striking partnership: Alan Shearer (left) watches as Michael Owen heads for gaol against Luxembourg.

Kevin Keegan is the man on whose shoulders the pressure falls; Alan Shearer, David Beckham, Tony Adams and David Seaman are the players whose skill will make or break the trip to Belgium and Holland.

England squeezed into the finals only after a narrow play-off victory over Scotland. Yet, in the event, qualifying at all was a minor triumph.

England had emerged from the 1998 FIFA World Cup with a sense of potential unfulfilled after the luckless shoot-out defeat by Argentina. European optimism was quickly dismissed, however, by a 2–1

defeat in Sweden during which midfielder Paul Ince was sent off. When coach Glenn Hoddle was forced out after making some offensive remarks about the handicapped, England were suddenly in crisis.

A brief interregnum under Howard Wilkinson, when England lost 2–0 to France at Wembley, provoked a public outcry for Keegan who was duly prised away from his rebuilding work at Fulham. Repairing the shattered morale of a national team is an even tougher job, as Keegan quickly discovered. He brought enormous optimism and confidence to the

Midfield maestro: Paul Scholes provided crucial qualifying goals.

task and said publicly that England could win the UEFA European Football Championship™, but performance did not live up to the promise.

In the end, England had to rely on Sweden beating nearest rivals Poland even to secure a place in the play-offs. Tension was racheted up to its tightest level when England were matched with the auld enemy, Scotland. Two goals from Paul Scholes brought victory over a poor Scottish side at Hampden Park but, back at Wembley, England were fortunate to escape with a 1–0 defeat. Only a superb reflex save by goalkeeper Seaman from Christian Dailly's late header sent England into the finals.

The fateful inevitability of being drawn in Group A alongside old rivals Germany – who had been pulled out of the FIFA World Cup hat with England five days earlier – stoked up fires for the drama ahead.

The paradox of England's position was underlined by Keegan when he said, "If you take the rankings, then I am manager of the weakest team in the group. But I know, with the players I've got, that I'm not manager of the weakest team. There's no reason, with the talent we've got, why we shouldn't get into the semi-finals … at least."

That talent starts with the Arsenal defensive nucleus of Seaman in goal and Adams and Martin Keown in central defence supported by the coveted Tottenham defender Sol Campbell. In midfield, England possess a balance between veteran enforcers such as Ince and David Batty and a creative attacker in Beckham. With top-scoring skipper Shearer and teenaged FIFA World Cup revelation Michael Owen up front, it becomes easier to understand Keegan's optimism, especially if all his men rise to the occasion.

COACH

Kevin Keegan

Born: 14 February 1951
Appointed: March 1999
Career: Keegan was an outstanding forward in the late 1970s and early 1980s when he was twice voted European Footballer of the Year. He won almost all the top prizes with Liverpool, then played in Germany for Hamburg before returning to England to play for Southampton and Newcastle. He quit football altogether on retiring but was tempted back to manage Newcastle which he did with extraordinary success. After resigning from Newcastle, he was persuaded by Harrods' owner Mohammed Al Fayed to mastermind the reawakening of Fulham and only left there to become England manager, a popular choice for the job in succession to Glenn Hoddle.

Slovenia

Slovenia are the rank outsiders of EURO 2000™, their place in the finals representing an extraordinary achievement for a national team competing in the UEFA European Football Championship™ for only the second time.

First of all, it was a surprise to continental football when they reached the play-offs, a greater surprise when they won 2–1 at home to Ukraine in the first leg and a major shock when they forged a 1–1 draw in Kiev to qualify for the finals 2–1 on aggregate.

The Slovenes are the youngest nation at the finals; it was only at the start of the 1990s that Slovenia slipped comparatively quietly out of the former Yugoslavia. A national championship was launched in 1991–92 and Olimpija Ljubljana have won the league title in every one of the first four years. The capital, Ljubljana, is the centre of domestic football, although Maribor have come to the fore in the last three seasons and their presence in the UEFA Champions League in the 1999–2000 season should, perhaps, have warned observers and opponents alike not to underestimate Slovenia at national team level.

In sports terms, tiny Slovenia, with its population of little more than two million people, means winter sports, especially skiing. But it has produced a handful of outstanding footballers down the years including, notably, Srecko Katanec. He starred as a wing-half or midfielder with Partizan Belgrade and then with Sampdoria of Genoa in Italy under Vujadin Boskov who is national coach of EURO 2000™ finals rivals and neighbours Yugoslavia.

Katanec has re-emerged as national coach and a man who is quick to snap back at suggestions that Slovenia are fortunate to have come so far, so soon. He

Fast forward: Red Star Belgrade's Milenko Acimovic.

COACH

Srecko Katanec

Born: 16 July 1973
Appointed: July 1998
Career: Katanec, an outstanding wing-half or all-purpose midfielder, began his playing career with top Slovene club Olimpija Ljubljana in the former Yugoslavia. He transferred up the domestic ladder with Dinamo Zagreb and army club Partizan Belgrade from where Italy's Sampdoria signed him in 1988. He starred for five years alongside Gianluca Vialli and Roberto Mancini before returning home to the independent Slovenia as coach of HIT Gorica. He succeeded Zdenko Verdenik as national coach in the summer of 1998.

New kids on the block: Slovenia will be making their debut at the UEFA European Football Championship™ finals.

says, "We deserved to qualify because we worked hard for it, we played well and we were brave enough to take risks. Fortune favours the brave, doesn't it? I think so. That is why I have taught my players that team spirit is what matters the most. It is important that all the players – even those on the bench – are fully motivated throughout the ninety minutes. We have to be strong friends – and strong-hearted."

In their qualifying group, Slovenia began erratically with a 2–2 draw away to Greece followed by a 2–1 home defeat by Norway. They picked up points against Latvia, Albania and Georgia and qualified for the play-offs with a match to spare. That was fortunate because they lost that last match by 3–0 at home to the Greeks who had emerged as their closest rivals. In the event, Slovenia finished two points ahead of them.

The one Slovene player with an international reputation is forward Zlatko Zahovic. He made his name in Portugal with FC Porto, then transferred to Greece with Olympiakos, for whom he starred in the UEFA Champions League last autumn. A row with their coach Dusan Bajevic led to Zahovic squabbling, also, with the club but Katanec expects all Zahovic's

problems to have been resolved by the time EURO 2000™ comes around. Katanec needs Zahovic clear in his mind to concentrate on attacking the defences of group rivals Spain, Norway and Yugoslavia.

In support of Zahovic will be Maribor goalkeeper Marko Simeunovic, his Belgian-based deputy Mladen Dabanovic – the Lokeren man who starred in the play-offs against Ukraine – midfielder Amir Karic, nicknamed "The Bulldozer", and support forward Milenko Acimovic from Red Star Belgrade. Acimovic scored a remarkable 50-metre goal in the first leg of the play-off victory over Ukraine.

European Championship Record

1960: Did not enter	**1980**: Did not enter
1964: Did not enter	**1984**: Did not enter
1968: Did not enter	**1988**: Did not enter
1972: Did not enter	**1992**: Did not enter
1976: Did not enter	**1996**: Did not qualify

Turkey

Turkey's political progress towards the European Union has been mirrored in football terms. Reaching the European finals in 1996 might have been considered a one-off, but Turkey's success in retaining their place among the élite proves it was far more than that.

Finals return: Turkey's playmaker Okan Buruk.

Indeed, the Turks felt unlucky not to have qualified directly for the finals rather than having to endure a tough play-off against the Republic of Ireland. As national coach Mustafa Denizli said before the Irish matches, "After beating and drawing with Germany in the qualifiers we really deserve to be in the finals already."

In fact, the Turks squandered their chance of finishing ahead of the Germans by losing concentration and vital points away to Finland and Moldova. That meant they finished two points behind Germany and became embroiled with the Irish. The first leg, in Dublin, ended in a 1–1 draw. Robbie Keane shot Ireland ahead in the 79th minute but an unnecessary handball by Lee Carsley presented the Turks with a penalty four minutes later which Tayfur converted.

That meant that a goalless draw back in Turkey would be enough to send them through on the away goals rule. The match was played in Bursa, a happy home for Turkey after victories there over Holland in 1997 and Germany in 1998. They did not win this time but a 0–0 draw was good enough to win the tie albeit

European Championship Record

1960: Did not qualify	**1980**: Did not qualify
1964: Did not qualify	**1984**: Did not qualify
1968: Did not qualify	**1988**: Did not qualify
1972: Did not qualify	**1992**: Did not qualify
1976: Did not qualify	**1996**: First round

On their way: Turkey line up before their play-off triumph over the Republic of Ireland.

with some unpleasant scenes as tempers boiled over in the closing stages.

The Turkish players dedicated their victory to the 18,000 victims of the earthquakes that had shocked the entire continent earlier in the year and also in the days leading up to the play-off. Now, rewarded with around £120,000 each in cash and cars, Turkey's stars go to the finals intent on improving on their performance at Euro 96 when they lost all their first-round matches and failed to score even one goal.

Denizli, in his second spell as national coach, has appealed for the entire nation to get behind the team – meaning, in particular, some people in the media who have criticized his selection policies. Denizli is happy with the nucleus of the team, from goalkeeper Rustu Recber who was first choice in 1996 in England, to playmaker Okan Buruk through to winger Arif Erdem and striker Hakan Sukur, who remains the Turks' outstanding player.

Okan first vaulted into the national team when he was 19, in a qualifier for the 1994 FIFA World Cup. Unhappily, it was also his last international appearance for six years – he broke a leg in the spring of 1993 and when he returned to action, lacked all the form and confidence of his teenage years. Only now is he at last

fulfilling his boyhood potential.

Hakan played once briefly in Italy with Torino but soon hurried home. Gaining confidence is the key to Turkey's progress up the international football ladder. Top club Galatasaray are regular contenders in the UEFA Champions League and foreign clubs are starting to take a serious interest in scouting the Turkish league for likely talent. They will be keeping a sharp eye on Turkey's progress in the EURO 2000™ finals.

COACH

Mustafa Denizli

Born: 10 November 1949
Appointed: August 1996
Career: A popular centre-forward in the Turkish domestic game in the 1970s, Denizli spent 18 years with Altay Izmir, for whom he was once top scorer in the league. He scored twice in 10 appearances for the national team and ended his playing career with Galatasaray. He was appointed as number two to German coach Jupp Derwall at Galatasaray and succeeded him with league title-winning success. Denizli was briefly national coach in 1987–88. He coached second division German club Allemagne Aachen before returning to Galatasaray in 1990. He succeeded Fatih Terim as national coach after Euro 96.

Battle of Britain winner: Paul Gascoigne scores for England against Scotland at Euro 96.

The Stars

Great players perform at their best on the great stages and the European game provides no higher platform than the finals of the UEFA European Football Championship™. Each succeeding tournament has added to the chapter of legends.

Soviet Union goalkeeper Lev Yashin was the championship's original hero back in 1960 when his spectacularly secure style not only earned his country the honour of being first champions but brought him the European Footballer of the Year award. In 1964 Luis Suarez of Spain stamped his playmaking authority on the event and Yugoslavia's Dragan Dzajic more than justified his "Magic Dragan" nickname in 1968.

Franz Beckenbauer and Gunter Netzer weaved dazzling midfield patterns for winners West Germany in 1972 and Antonin Panenka sealed ultimate glory with the cheekiest penalty of all four years later. Karl-Heinz Rummenigge was head and shoulders above the rest in 1980, while Michel Platini was a colossus for France as they delighted their fans and thrilled the rest of watching Europe in their homeland in 1984.

Marco Van Basten and Ruud Gullit transferred their brilliant Milan partnership to Holland's cause in 1988 and in 1992 Peter Schmeichel, Michael Laudrup and the surprise package from Denmark exploded on to the stage with victory over the German favourites. Four more years and Paul Gascoigne scored a memorable goal in remarkable circumstances for England against Scotland at Wembley in the Battle of Britain.

Now, any number of candidates may join these veteran heroes in the history books.

Marc Wilmots

Belgium

Belgium have not been in the UEFA European Football Championship™ finals since 1984, and Marc Wilmots is relishing playing host. "It will be an historic event," he says. "We first staged the finals in 1972. We have waited a long time for them to come back. We cannot waste this chance."

Such determination is characteristic of the man nicknamed the "Wild Boar". He did not flinch in stepping up to score the penalty in the shoot-out that won his club, Schalke, the UEFA Cup in 1997.

Wilmots joined Schalke in 1994, soon after he and his country had been controversially knocked out of the FIFA World Cup by Germany. Wilmots settled to an attacking midfield role which proved particularly productive in the triumphant UEFA Cup run. Wilmots scored five goals, including the crucial one in the first leg of the final against Internazionale.

Wilmots began his professional career at 16 with Belgian club Saint-Trond before moving on to former Cup-Winners' Cup holders Mechelen. In these early stages of his career Wilmots used to play as an out-and-out striker. It was in this position that he made his debut for Belgium at 21 in 1990 but was left on the substitutes' bench throughout the FIFA World Cup in Italy.

He helped Mechelen to runners-up positions in both the League and the Cup, and actually won the Belgian Cup in 1993 with Standard Liège.

Under previous coach Georges Leekens Wilmots was captain of the national side. However, under new man Robert Waseige there seems to be some doubt about whether he will skipper the side for EURO 2000™. Recently, Lorenzo Staelens of Anderlecht, the most senior player in the team, has been wearing the armband. For Wilmots such uncertainties are not his main concern. He says, "All I have to worry about is concentrating on my football and making sure I play well enough to earn my place in the squad under the new manager."

Wilmots: sometime skipper.

FACTFILE

Position	: Midfield
Club	: Schalke (Germany)
Previous clubs	: Saint-Trond, Mechelen, Standard Liège
Born	: 22 February 1969
Intl apps	: 43
Intl goals	: 16

"If I had eleven players like Wilmots in my team I could take on anybody, anywhere. He is absolutely fearless"

Georges Leekens
former Belgium manager

Patrik Berger

Czech Republic

The greatest natural talent discovered in Czech football in the 1990s, Patrik Berger hit the international stage in his country's remarkable progress at Euro 96. In the Czech Republic's first international finals as an independent state, he scored four times in the qualifying campaign as well as netting their only goal from a penalty in the final defeat against Germany.

Berger started his career in the youth sections of Sparta Prague, but they did not offer him a professional contract. Local rivals Slavia Prague, however, were sufficiently impressed and he began his professional career with them. Having twice been runner-up in the Czech league with Slavia – to Sparta – Berger transferred to Borussia Dortmund in 1995. He spent just one year in Germany, but played a key role as Dortmund progressed to the semi-finals of the European Champions League. He crossed paths with Sparta again, as they were eliminated from Dortmund's group.

Despite his success in the qualifying event, Berger was not a regular member of the team that played in the last UEFA European Football Championship™. Like his teammates, he was devastated not to qualify for the FIFA World Cup – with around 40 caps for his country he had wanted to play against non-European opposition.

What is for sure is that Berger will take second stage to no one in this Championship. He is now established as a key member of the attacking line-up. Added to this, the 1998–99 season was easily his most accomplished at Liverpool, the club he joined in the summer of 1996. After an explosive start to his Anfield career, scoring four stunning goals in two games in September 1996, he drifted in and out of the side. With new Liverpool manager Gerard Houllier Berger seems to have found the consistency he lacked for so long.

Berger can fit into attack or midfield, preferring to play on the left-hand side. He passes the ball well, links the play with his direct running and has a superb shot, which he is always keen to employ. The two free kicks he scored against Estonia in qualifying were spectacular examples of the danger he will pose to goalkeepers in EURO 2000™.

"All you ask of a player is that he makes himself indispensable to your team. Berger did that at Euro 96"

Dusan Uhrin,
former national coach

★ FACTFILE ★

Position	: Midfield/forward
Club	: Liverpool (England)
Previous clubs	: Slavia, Sparta, Borussia Dortmund (Germany)
Born	: 10 November 1973
Intl apps	: 37
Intl goals	: 17

Berger: free kick expert.

Lilian Thuram

France

In all the hype following France's victory at the 1998 FIFA World Cup, with the glamour names of Zidane and Petit being lauded, it was easy to forget the right-back who scored the semi-final goals against Croatia and provided much, much more, which took France to the final.

Not that Lilian Thuram will mind too much. With his wire-rimmed spectacles and conservative dress, friends and admirers feel he will never quite make the celebrity pages. But they also know – as many believe – that he is the best defender in the world.

Thuram grew up studying the skills of the French mid-field platform that won them the 1984 UEFA European Football Championship™. Originally, he wanted to be a mixture of Tigana and Platini, and it was as a midfielder that he was discovered by Monaco aged 18 years. Not considered mature enough, Thuram missed Monaco's French Cup win in 1991 and the 1992 Cup-Winners' Cup final defeat. But in the 1992–93 season he shone in his now favoured position of centre-back, missing only one league game and forcing his way into the national squad.

The disappointment of Euro 96 was unfair on Thuram and his defensive team-mates. They did their job – it was the forwards who could not score enough goals. Parma recognized as much and signed Thuram that summer.

In Italy, he is regularly voted one of the best foreign players in *Serie A* by the Italian media and experts. He mixes great pace in recovery with a rugged assurance in the tackle and a deft accuracy with both long and short passes. He was a rock in Parma's UEFA Cup-winning side in 1998–99. The team also qualified for the Champions League.

The highs of the FIFA World Cup have not lulled Thuram into complacency. He knows you are only as good as your next game, or in international terms, your next tournament – "When I go out to play another match I want to win. I never think, 'I won the World Cup so I don't need to bother anymore.' A footballer wants to win every game; at least, I hope so. If not, he had better find another occupation."

Thuram: rock of Parma.

★ FACTFILE ★

Position	: Defender
Club	: Parma (Italy)
Previous clubs	: Monaco
Born	: 1 January 1972
Intl apps	: 51
Intl goals	: 2

"It's easy to be a forward, enjoying yourself in attack, when you know Lilian Thuram is behind you in defence"

Zinedine Zidane,
France World Cup-winning team-mate

Zinedine Zidane

France

Three other great French footballers have been hailed as European Footballer of the Year before Zinedine Zidane, but he can lay claim to being the greatest of them all.

Zidane: World Cup hero.

Raymond Kopa collected his prize in 1958 for inspiring Les Bleus to third place in the FIFA World Cup. Michel Platini won a hat-trick of awards in the mid 1980s. Jean-Pierre Papin claimed the honour with Marseille.

But Zidane is different. None of the others can boast a World Cup-winner's medal. Not only that, he headed two decisive goals in France's 3–0 win over Brazil in the 1998 final.

Zidane, the son of Algerian immigrants, grew up in Marseille but, oddly, escaped the attentions of the club on his doorstep. Instead, he made his professional debut with Cannes and then joined Bordeaux with whom he reached the 1996 UEFA Cup final. He was also on the losing side in two successive Champions League finals with Juventus before his FIFA World Cup victory.

Zidane made his explosive international debut in August 1994 as a substitute against the Czech Republic. He scored two stunning goals in the final 10 minutes to rescue a 2–2 draw and his presence at the heart of the action has never been questioned since then.

Zidane found the FIFA World Cup had its own frustrations; he was sent off against Saudi Arabia in France's second match and could only watch while his team-mates squeezed past Paraguay in the second round by virtue of Laurent Blanc's golden goal. National coach Aimé Jacquet consoled him by saying, "Zizou, the French team are not just you. But what I do know is that it's you who'll make us win."

Back against his adopted homeland of Italy, Zidane nervelessly converted the first penalty in France's shoot-out success. Semi-final victory over Croatia prepared the stage for Zidane's virtuoso match-winning display in the final triumph over Brazil. Both his goals, unusually, were headers.

It was inevitable that he would be crowned European Footballer of the Year with almost 200 more votes than runner-up Davor Suker of Croatia. In the spring of 1999 Zidane also collected FIFA's World Player trophy. No wonder he says, "I've got used to being a winner and it's a great feeling. You want it to go on … and on … and on."

> **"Zizou has everything it takes to be a great player, plus he is also a very genuine human being. It's a rare mixture"**
>
> Michel Platini, French former player

★ FACTFILE ★

Position	: Midfield
Club	: Juventus (Italy)
Previous clubs	: Cannes, Bordeaux
Born	: 23 June 1972
Intl apps	: 49
Intl goals	: 12

Oliver Bierhoff
Germany

Oliver Bierhoff will do well to top his performance in Euro 96 – it was his golden goal which won Germany the title. Yet he was not originally a key member of the squad, coming on as a substitute to score that famous goal.

Since then he has gone from strength to strength, becoming his country's captain and a leading figure in Milan's Italian championship-winning side. Bierhoff moved from Udinese to Milan and coach Alberto Zaccheroni seems able to draw the best from him. Despite problems settling in and disagreements over tactics, Bierhoff still managed to score more goals for Milan in one season than any other forward since Marco Van Basten. Though keen to point out the number of assists he gets, Bierhoff knows well what he does best – he scores goals.

He tries to distance himself from comparisons with other top strikers such as Ronaldo, Alex Del Piero or Gabriel Batistuta by saying, "I'm not a spectacular striker. I score simple goals." This supposedly "unspectacular" style has nevertheless proved fruitful – he was Serie A top scorer with Udinese in 1998, scoring 27 goals in 32 appearances, following that with 20 in his first season with Milan.

Germany may have reached the quarter-finals of France 98, but it was a generally lacklustre team performance. Regardless of this, Bierhoff still managed to score three goals and enhance his own reputation. He recognizes the need to change direction, saying, "There

have been a lot of changes. Now we have to rebuild for the future. It is a new era for Germany."

The kind of pressure that classes reaching the quarter-finals of the FIFA World Cup a failure is something Bierhoff feels keenly, both at domestic and international level. He says, "I feel this pressure every day. Through the television at home when I get up in the morning, from the newspapers, from the journalists at the training ground. Everywhere. The fans are always wanting something."

This pressure is not a negative force, more of a challenge. The sense of responsibility Bierhoff feels for the overall team performance makes him an ideal captain; above all he wants to help the team to do well.

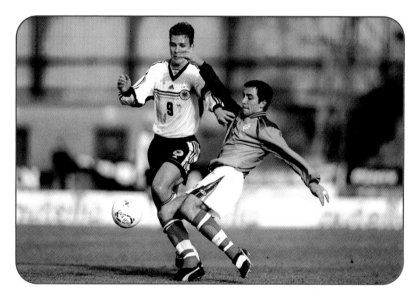

Bierhoff: golden goals.

★ FACTFILE ★

Position	: Centre-forward
Club	AC Milan (Italy)
Previous clubs	SW Essen, Uerdingen, Hamburg, Udinese (Italy)
Born	: 1 May 1968
Intl apps	: 44
Intl goals	: 25

"Not all strikers make good leaders or captains. Bierhoff is just that – it's what makes him different"

Erich Ribbeck,
Germany's national coach

Lothar Matthäus

Germany

Lothar Matthäus will make one of the longest trips to drive Germany into the UEFA European Football Championship™ finals.

This spring he left Bayern Munich to take up up a contract with New York-New Jersey MetroStars in Major League Soccer in the United States.

Most European players see the flight stateside as a gentle prelude to retirement but Matthäus is different. Never, at any stage in his entire career, has the world's record international – with nearly 150 caps to his name – ever taken anything gently.

As national coach Erich Ribbeck says: "With a player like Matthäus, age is not an issue. He has experience, ambition and a wonderful will-to-win. Any coach wants those qualities in his players. It's remarkable that Matthäus has played that way all through his career – even now that he is approaching forty."

Matthäus, midfielder turned sweeper, has won just about everything in the game since abandoning a teenage apprenticeship as an interior designer and decorator. Even then Matthäus never suffered fools gladly and a number of bookings and suspensions for a wayward temper cost Matthäus representative opportunities with the Bavarian youth team.

These were not qualities, however, which professional clubs would overlook. Sure enough, Matthäus was snapped up by Borussia Mönchen-gladbach, moving on upward to rivals Bayern Munich in 1984 – after Matthäus had missed a penalty in Borussia's cup final defeat at the hands of ... Bayern.

Matthäus became, with Bayern, three times champion of West Germany, won the cup once and collected a runners-up medal in the European Champions Cup, when Bayern were surprisingly beaten in the 1987 final by FC Porto. But the occasional defeat did not dent his reputation. Italian giants Inter proved that in 1988 when they stepped in to pay Bayern £2.5million for him.

With Matthäus at the midfield helm, Inter won the Italian league and the UEFA Cup and he skippered Germany to victory – also in Italy, of course - in the 1990 FIFA World Cup finals before returning to Germany to earn more domestic titles with Bayern.

Now he was no longer the midfield dynamo but the attacking sweeper. Injuries took their toll. Matthäus was bitterly upset to miss the 1992 UEFA European Championship™ finals in which Germany suffered a shock Final defeat by Denmark. He was also furious at the way some of his team-mates capitulated in the quarter-finals of the FIFA World Cup in both 1994 (to Bulgaria) and in 1998 (to Croatia).

The rest of Europe should be warned: Matthäus intends to go out in glory.

> **"With a player like Matthäus, age is not an issue. He has experience, ambition and a wonderful will-to-win"**
>
> Erich Ribbeck, Germany's national coach.

Matthaus: back from injury.

★ FACTFILE ★

Position	: Sweeper
Club	: Bayern Munich, New York-New Jersey MetroStars (US)
Previous clubs	: Borussia Mönchengladbach, Bayern Munich, Internazionale (Italy)
Born	: 21 March 1961
Intl apps	: 143
Intl goals	: 22

Dennis Bergkamp

The *Netherlands*

At the 1998 FIFA World Cup in France Dennis Bergkamp set a Dutch international scoring record. He smashed home his 36th goal for Holland in spectacular style, overtaking Faas Wilkes's tally, as Holland beat Argentina in the dying minutes of their quarter-final. Most of these goals have come from Bergkamp's favoured position, playing just behind the main striker.

Bergkamp: goal scoring records

Bergkamp celebrated a similarly successful FIFA World Cup in 1994 when he scored three goals to help the Dutch to a quarter-final place. He was also named in the tournament's all-star team. The unfortunate fall-out from that summer was the bomb hoax that provoked his fear of flying.

One of the most appealing aspects of Bergkamp's game is that he does not simply score goals – he scores great goals. He is the only player to scoop first, second and third places in *Match of the Day*'s Goal of the Month competition, which he did in 1997. It was form such as this that helped guide Arsenal to their second League and Cup double.

Bergkamp, like so many other Dutch greats, graduated through the ranks of Ajax's youth training scheme. Making his debut at 17, Bergkamp displayed technical skills and an eye for goal that quickly earned him comparisons with former Ajax stars Johan Cruyff and Marco Van Basten. In 1988 he set a Dutch league record of scoring in 10 consecutive games. Bergkamp helped Ajax to victory in the UEFA Cup in 1992 and scored three goals in the UEFA European Football Championship™ finals the same year, though Holland lost their semi-final to Denmark on penalties.

Although he won the UEFA Cup, his spell at Inter was not a happy one. He was expected to fill the position of all-out front man. It was clearly a role in which he was not comfortable and, amid much criticism, the goals dried up and he looked a shadow of his former self.

His transfer to Arsenal in the summer of 1995 heralded a new dawn and he quickly became revered and respected not only at Highbury but throughout England.

This culminated in his winning both the writers' and players' player of the year trophies in 1998.

Coming back from France 98, Bergkamp seemed a little jaded. Doubts were raised over his temperament, with niggling arguments and elbows flying. Despite this, his immaculate control and finishing make him a vital part of both Arsene Wenger's and Frank Rijkaard's squads.

"I can't believe, with such talent, that Dennis Bergkamp is really from this planet"

Louis Van Gaal, Barcelona coach

FACTFILE

Position	: Striker
Club	: Arsenal (England)
Previous clubs	: Ajax, Internazionale (Italy)
Born	: 10 May 1969
Intl apps	: 70
Intl goals	: 36

Edgar Davids

The Netherlands

One of Frank Rijkaard's first acts as Dutch coach was to promote Edgar Davids to vice-captain in a move that surprised many. Davids's international career is notable as much for his being sent home in disgrace from Euro 96 as for his performances in Holland's flowing attacking football of France 98.

His public bust-up with then coach Gus Hiddink forced him into the international wilderness for two years before he was recalled for the FIFA World Cup. His industrious midfield work played a huge role in taking Holland on to fourth place, having lost to Brazil on penalties in the semifinals.

Davids is, like many of the young Dutch stars, a graduate of the Ajax academy of football intellectuals but he has a fire in him that no one has been able to control. Soon after his transfer to Milan, in the summer of 1996, Davids stopped his Porsche at traffic lights and it was attacked by two would-be muggers. Instead of driving off, Davids stepped out of the car and gave both a beating.

His time at Milan followed a turbulent course as the club continued their freefall descent. Davids broke his leg in his first season, which ruled him out for six months. Davids is not too proud to admit a lesson sorely learned, saying, "Going to Milan was a big mistake. It was a bad time, the most bitter experience of my club career. But I have tried to use it in a positive way. It has allowed me to change and mature as a person. It taught me that being a world-class footballer is about being in control."

This mature viewpoint may have had a lot to do with his

Davids: fighting qualities.

international recall. It certainly helped him play a vital role in Juventus' championship-winning side of 1998. The team also reached the Champions Cup final, losing to Real Madrid.

In fact, it could be said that Davids has done well not to fall into the too much too young, wasted potential mould. By the time he was 24 he had won the Champions Cup, the European Super Cup, the UEFA Cup, the World Club Cup, three Dutch league titles and one Dutch Cup. Davids is not comfortable resting on such past glories. He says, "The higher the stakes, the tougher the fight, the more fired up I get. I can deliver. I am a winner."

That is something the Dutch, more often than not the nearly men of international football, would love to hear him say come the end of EURO 2000™.

> **"Every time I play against Davids at club level I wish more and more that he was back on my side again"**
>
> Clarence Seedorf,
> Holland team-mate

★ FACTFILE ★

Position	: Midfield
Club	: Juventus (Italy)
Previous clubs	: Ajax, Milan (Italy)
Born	: 13 March 1973
Intl apps	: 25
Intl goals	: 4

Paolo Maldini

Italy

Throughout the 1990s Paolo Maldini has been considered one of the best defenders in the world. He is a regular in fantasy World XI teams.

Captain of both club and country, Maldini has no international winners' medals to go with his 100 plus caps. He won a third-place medal in the 1990 FIFA World Cup, but the closest he came was the agonizing defeat on penalties in the 1994 final. He admits it was difficult to get over that disappointment, accounting for, by his high standards, a relatively poor subsequent season for Milan. Coach Fabio Capello even accused him of lacking charisma after the Cup final defeat by Lazio. Interesting to note that it is Maldini who is still at Milan.

In his second season as Milan captain, however, Maldini led the spectacular charge to the championship title in 1998–99. Club vice-president Adriano Gallani is in no doubt about the reason for Milan's recovery – "At the base of this successful season lies the fact that Paolo is finally captain of Milan. His moral leadership of the team is now unquestioned and his repair work in the dressing room is bearing copious fruit." Coach Alberto Zaccheroni agrees. It is simply taken for granted now that Maldini is a great player.

His debut for Milan came at the very early age of 16 – all the more surprising in Italy, where players generally do not get into the first team until they are in their early 20s. He has won six Italian league titles and three European

Champions Cups to date. His international debut came at the similarly early age of 19. He first starred in the 1988 UEFA European Football Championship™ finals in West Germany, soon becoming a permanent fixture on the international scene.

Paolo has long since grown out of the shadow of his father, Cesare. He is taller, leaner and quicker and has already far outstripped him in terms of international appearances. But he never forgets the influence his father had on him, saying, "My father taught me everything. I wanted to succeed for myself but I owed it to him."

Cesare, also a European Cup-winning captain and key defender with Milan, has been Paolo's coach at both Under-21 and full international level.

This could be Maldini's last chance to win a senior national team competition. It would be a more than fitting reward for such a distinguished player.

Maldini: family fortunes.

"Paolo never gives up, even in training matches. It's astonishing"

Alberto Zaccheroni,
Milan coach

★ FACTFILE ★	
Position	: Left-back/centre-back
Club	: AC Milan
Previous clubs	: none
Born	: 26 June 1968
Intl apps	: 103
Intl goals	: 7

Christian Vieri

Italy

Vieri: world record fee.

In his last three transfers Christian Vieri has cost Atlético Madrid, Lazio and Internazionale a total of £61 million. The Vatican newspaper said that his £31 million transfer to Inter "insulted the poor". Vieri himself does not see money as a huge issue – "When I go out on to the pitch I don't think about things like that."

What he does think about is scoring goals, something he has done consistently at every one of his eight clubs over the last eight years. In his single season at Atlético Madrid he scored 24 goals in 24 games, convincing Lazio to shell out £18 million. His form for Lazio in his one season there was enough to boost his value by £13 million – an offer they could not refuse.

The speed with which Vieri's valuation has soared is in contrast to what could be seen as a comparatively slow development through junior ranks at Torino, then Serie B clubs Pisa, Ravenna and Venezia. There were those who felt his place owed more to the fact that his father was a former professional rather than to his own potential. He burst out of his father's shadow in 1995, scoring seven goals in 19 games for Atalanta in *Serie A*. At the end of his first year he moved to Juventus, a club who have been trying unsuccessfully to re-sign him ever since they let him go a season later.

When first choice Juve striker Alen Boksic was injured, Vieri took centre stage in their Champions League run, which ended in the surprise defeat by Borussia Dortmund in the final.

Despite making a four-fold profit on Vieri, the decision to sell him to Atlético was later referred to as "foolishness" by Juve owner Gianni Agnelli. Vieri, characteristically, seemed unfazed by the hype and chalked up a goal a game before shining for Italy in the 1998 FIFA World Cup finals, ending as their top scorer with five goals.

Each of the last few seasons has loaded more challenges and pressure on to Vieri, and he has responded with goals each time. This focus and ability to rise to the occasion make him vital to Italy's challenge, particularly after their disappointing performances in the competition in 1996. Matched with this is Vieri's own confidence in his team-mates. He says, "We are the best team in the world."

Coach Dino Zoff sees Vieri as a complete forward. He says, "Vieri may be big and strong and good in the air but he is surprisingly nimble on the ground, as plenty of defenders have found to their cost!"

★ FACTFILE ★

Position	: **Centre-forward**
Club	: **Internazionale**
Previous clubs	: **Prato, Torino, Pisa, Ravenna, Venezia, Atalanta, Juventus, Atlético Madrid (Spain), Lazio**
Born	: **12 July 1973**
Intl apps	: **19**
Intl goals	: **10**

"Vieri may be big and strong and good in the air but he is surprisingly nimble on the ground, too"

Dino Zoff, Italy coach

Tore Andre Flo
Norway

Tore Andre Flo, while often frustrated by the rotation system used at star-flooded Chelsea, remains central to Norway's hopes of progress at the UEFA European Football Championship™.

Standing a huge six foot four, heading ability is Flo's main talent, but this belies a neat touch on the ground. As well as challenging defenders as a target man, he likes to drop into midfield, using his dribbling skills to create chances for himself and others. His well-rounded forward play has added a new and exciting dimension to a Norwegian attack previously famed for an over-dependence on kick and run.

The initial highlight of Flo's international career was the 4–2 upset win over Brazil in a friendly in 1997. Flo shot to world prominence with two of the goals against the then world champions. He described the feeling as "simply incredible". He went one better the following year, inspiring Norway's victory against Brazil in the 1998 FIFA World Cup. He scored the first goal and was fouled for the penalty converted by Kjetil Rekdal in their surprise 2–1 win.

Flo started his career with Tromsø before moving to SK Brann, for whom he impressed in their UEFA Cup matches against Liverpool in 1996. He joined Chelsea for a bargain £300,000 in the summer of 1997, and was instrumental in their charge on the League Cup, Cup-Winners' Cup and, this season, the Champions League.

Flo: new dimension.

The story could have been very different if Joe Royle had got his way on transfer deadline day in 1997. He wanted to sign Flo for Everton, but chairman Peter Johnson felt he was not good enough and the disagreement ended with Royle losing his job.

The quality of attacking players at Chelsea boss Gianluca Vialli's disposal – Gianfranco Zola, Gustavo Poyet, Chris Sutton – has limited Flo's chances at English domestic level. But he has often proved highly effective as a substitute, as shown by the match with Blackburn last season. Trailing 3–2 with 10 minutes to go, Flo came on to score two brilliant goals in three minutes, giving Chelsea their first league victory at Ewood Park for 22 years.

Norway's recent form in qualifying has been immense; they won eight out of their 10 matches in reaching EURO 2000™. Former coach Egil Olsen has no doubts about Flo's ability to perform at the highest levels, saying, "For me, Tore Andre is among the best in the world."

★ FACTFILE

Position	: Centre-forward
Club	: Chelsea (England)
Previous clubs	: Sogndal, Tromsø, Brann Bergen
Born	: 15 June 1973
Intl apps	: 43
Intl goals	: 21

"Tore Andre Flo is seriously underrated. For me, [he] is among the best in the world"

Egil Olsen,
Norway's 1998 FIFA World Cup coach

Manuel Rui Costa

Portugal

Portugal has produced a stream of wonderfully gifted players down the years but many have failed to lift that talent beyond their own borders when lured away by lucrative contracts in Spain or Italy – not so Manuel Rui Costa.

Rui Costa: play-maker supreme.

The guiding star of the national team's midfield in the forth-coming finals of the UEFA European Football Championship™ has been one of the out-standing talents on view in *Serie A* ever since he signed for the Florence club Fiorentina in the summer of 1994. Indeed, for all the fuss over the goals of Gabriel Batistuta, the Argentine centre-forward would be the first to point to Rui Costa as a key partner in penalty-box crime.

Rui Costa was marked out for a great future while still only 14 and a precocious youth talent. He was fortunate to come under the wing of Carlos Queiros who had been charged by the Portuguese federation with building a productive youth policy. Under Queiros Portugal had been FIFA World Youth Cup winners in 1989 and, with Rui Costa in a starring role, they repeated the trick in 1991. Playing in front of their own fans, Portugal beat Argentina, the Irish Republic and South Korea in their first-round group, then Mexico 2–1 after extra time in the quarter-finals. Rui Costa played midfield anchor-man and contributed the single decisive goal when Portugal defeated Australia 1–0 in the semi-finals. The final, against Brazil, was played in front of the biggest crowd Rui Costa has ever confronted – some 130,000 in the newly expanded Benfica Stadium. It was goalless at 90 minutes and still goalless after extra time. Portugal led 3–2 in the penalty shoot-out when Brazil's Marquinhos fluffed his shot. Rui Costa, nervelessly, walked from the centre circle to place his own kick past keeper Roger and turn Portugal into world champions.

All the experience he has gained since then with Benfica and Fiorentina has not been enough for Rui Costa to repeat the trick at national team level. But many observers believe he, and Portugal, are good enough to prove the most dangerous outsiders at EURO 2000™.

At least his name will live on, whatever the outcome of these European finals and wherever Rui Costa's inventive talents may take him. In his honour, the oldest youth tournament back home in Portugal has been renamed the "Rui Costa Championship".

★ FACTFILE ★

Position	: Midfield
Club	: Fiorentina (Italy)
Previous clubs	: Fafe, Benfica
Born	: 29 March 1972
Intl apps	: 48
Intl goals	: 17

"He can pass to whomever he likes, wherever he likes, whenever he likes, and always with millimetre perfect accuracy"

Carlos Queiros
former Portugal coach

Gheorghe Hagi
Romania

"Gica" Hagi, the so-called "Maradona of the Carpathians", has been Romania's star of the last decade. The first to leave the country after the 1989 anti-communist revolution that knocked down political and sporting barriers, he has been the leading light and captain for half a decade.

Hagi began his career with local club, FC Constanta, and swiftly moved up the domestic ladder. He was brought to the Romanian capital by Sportul Studentesc, but was stolen away, on political orders, by the army club Steaua Bucharest.

His left foot has been compared with that of Hungarian great, Ferenc Puskas. It brought him 100 league goals while still a teenager. He was twice the league's leading marksman and scored 76 goals in 97 league games before joining Real Madrid for a Romanian record £2 million after the 1990 FIFA World Cup.

Hagi did not take well to Spanish football. In his first season he scored only three goals, disappointing fans and management alike. His second season tally of 14 was not enough to win Madrid the title, and they were content to let him go to promoted Brescia in Italy. There, alongside fellow Romanian internationals Dorin Mateut, Ioan Sabau and Florin Raducioiu, Hagi fitted in well. He says, "I loved the place. All my friends were there."

After the FIFA World Cup of 1994 it was clear that Brescia would not hold on to Hagi for long. He scored an astonishingly long, angled lob from out near the left touchline in the opening game against Colombia. It began a remarkable sequence that earned him a place in almost everyone's team of the tournament. His form was rewarded with a lucrative transfer to Barcelona.

Unfortunately, he suffered similar problems to his spell at Madrid. Team manager Johan Cruyff did not seem willing or able to fit his tactics to Hagi's style and he became an increasingly distant figure on the substitutes' bench. After two years he moved to Galatasaray of Turkey.

Despite his undoubted class Hagi's star has seemed to fade a little in recent years. Romania were embarrassingly last in their Euro 96 group and went out in the second round of France 98 with Hagi displaying none of his former brilliance. He even retired from the national team but found a recall to arms impossible to resist in the run-up to EURO 2000™.

The elder statesman of Romanian football, he is still as highly praised for his tactical as his technical ability. This is his last chance to shine in an international arena, one he will want to take after years building a reputation as brilliant yet inconsistent.

Haji: final fling

★ FACTFILE ★

Position	: Midfield
Club	: Galatasaray (Turkey)
Previous clubs	: Constanta, Sportul Studentesc, Steaua Bucharest, Real Madrid (Spain), Brescia (Italy), Barcelona (Spain)
Born	: 5 February 1965
IIntl apps	: 119
Intl goals	: 34

"Great players like Hagi cannot be coached. They are a force of nature"

Mircea Lucescu,
former Romania coach

Raul Gonzàlez

Spain

It is testament to Raul's importance in the current Spanish side that, when asked what the spine of his team would be, coach José Camacho instantly named a player still only 21 years of age.

Raul: Real breakthrough.

Yet it's not so surprising when you consider that in the 1998–99 season Raul was top scorer in the Spanish top division, scoring as many as fellow Madrid strikers Fernando Morientes and Savio put together. For a team with one of the worst defensive records in the whole division, Madrid would have been lost without Raul. As it was, they conceded 62 goals but still came second. Interestingly, Raul was the first Spanish player to win the Primera Liga's top-scorer trophy for seven years.

His form for Spain has been similarly electrifying. In March 1999 he scored seven goals in the space of four days for his country, four in the 9–0 drubbing of Austria, and a hat-trick in the 6–0 victory over San Marino. In total he scored an astonishing 11 goals in qualifying for EURO 2000™, as Spain recovered from the shock first-game defeat against Cyprus to win the group comfortably.

Raul started as a youth team player with Atlético Madrid but moved to Real when Atlético president Jesus Gil scrapped the youth team in order to save money. Atlético's short-sighted loss was Real's gain as Raul made his debut in 1994, helping them win the Spanish title in 1995 and 1997. On top of this, Real with Raul won both the Champions League and World Club Cup in 1998.

On the pitch Raul boasts complete forward skills. More confident with his left foot, he can nevertheless turn defenders all ways up. His game is difficult to read – seeming to shape for a blast at goal, he will suddenly launch a deft chip over a confused goalkeeper.

Off the pitch he is mild-mannered and generous. He visits sick children in his spare time, does not talk out of turn to the media and has even hosted a television show on the history of Real and Atlético Madrid with Atlético player José Caminero.

He says he owes his success to the first of his many coaches at Real, Jorge Valdano, but gives credit for recent form to Spain coach Camacho, saying, "He's convinced us we're winners again."

Spain have not been winners of a senior international prize since they won this competition in 1964. Still young, Raul will have plenty more opportunities but he may never have a better one.

> **"Our team leans on Hierro in defence, Guardiola in midfield and, of course, Raul in attack"**
>
> José Camacho,
> Spain coach

★ FACTFILE ★

Position	: Forward
Club	: Real Madrid
Previous clubs	: none
Born	: 27 June 1977
Intl apps	: 29
Intl goals	: 15

Stefan Schwarz

Sweden

Stefan Schwarz is now in his second spell in the English Premier League. Having spent a year with Arsenal in 1994–95, he joined Sunderland at the start of the 1999–2000 season.

Schwarz began his career with hometown club Kulldall before exiled English coach Roy Hodgson took him to Malmö in 1987. After a short spell with Bayer Leverkusen in Germany, he was bought by fellow Swede Sven-Goran Eriksson for Benfica in 1990. The thinking behind Eriksson's move was to unite Schwarz with international midfield partner Jonas Thern. The two had proved themselves a formidable central partnership in both the 1992 UEFA European Football Championship™ and the 1994 FIFA World Cup.

As hosts in 1992, the only time before now that Sweden have played in the Championship, they reached the semi-finals. They repeated the achievement in the FIFA World Cup finals two years later, eventually surprising many by finishing third.

Just before that FIFA World Cup Schwarz was signed by Arsenal for £1.8 million. He adapted well to the rigours of the Premier League, his combative skills working effectively in the fast-paced English game in which the midfield battle is often crucial. This defensive quality in his game fitted in well with Arsenal's style under George Graham. It was a surprise, therefore, that he lasted just a year before moving to Italy with Fiorentina – apparently he had not settled so well to the English lifestyle.

In his first season at Fiorentina he won the Italian Cup. He also scored in the second round of the following season's Cup-Winners' Cup as Fiorentina reached the semi-finals, where they were knocked out by Barcelona.

In 1998 he moved to Spain with Valencia, where he played in the team that lost out to Liverpool in the UEFA Cup second round on away goals. He scored four goals in his one season in Spain. On coming back to England he played a key part in newly promoted Sunderland's impressive start to life in the Premiership.

Now he comes to EURO 2000™ rated as one of the most experienced players at the entire event.

FACTFILE

Position	: Midfield
Club	: Sunderland (England)
Previous clubs	: Malmö, Benfica (Portugal), Arsenal (England), Fiorentina (Italy), Valencia (Spain)
Born	: 18 April 1969
Intl apps	: 64
Intl goals	: 6

**"He never stops running.
I don't know where he finds the energy"**

Tommy Svensson,
Sweden's 1994 FIFA World Cup manager

Schwarz: anchor man.

Sinisa Mihajlovic

Yugoslavia

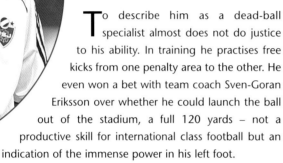

Sinisa Mihajlovic cuts a cheerful figure on the football pitch, often sporting a slight grin as he goes to take his infamous corners and free kicks. Defenders and goalkeepers could be forgiven for thinking that he is simply being malicious. His thunderbolt free kicks and curling corners are a nightmare to deal with.

Mihajlovic: national pride.

To describe him as a dead-ball specialist almost does not do justice to his ability. In training he practises free kicks from one penalty area to the other. He even won a bet with team coach Sven-Goran Eriksson over whether he could launch the ball out of the stadium, a full 120 yards – not a productive skill for international class football but an indication of the immense power in his left foot.

In his seven seasons in *Serie A* with Roma, Sampdoria and Lazio he has scored around 30 goals from free kicks. Included in this number is the torrid time he gave Sampdoria goalkeeper Fabrizio Ferron in Lazio's 5–2 win last season – Mihajlovic scored an amazing hat-trick of free kicks.

The product of a mixed family – Serb father, Croat mother – Mihajlovic has been profoundly affected by the strife in his home country. In a visit to his hometown, Vukovar, he was shocked at the scale of destruction, saying, "Vukovar was wiped out like some sort of Hiroshima, our house reduced to rubble."

He did not attempt to hide his feelings at NATO's bombing of his homeland last spring, wearing a black armband in memory of the victims.

After their poor showing at the 1998 FIFA World Cup

FACTFILE	
Position	: Sweeper
Club	: Lazio (Italy)
Previous clubs	: Vojvodina, Red Star Belgrade, Roma (Italy), Sampdoria (Italy)
Born	: 20 February 1969
Intl apps	: 41
Intl goals	: 5

finals in France, critics suggested that Yugoslavia would not qualify for EURO 2000™. Mihajlovic obviously disagreed and argued that the players felt they had something to prove – and prove it they did. Mihajlovic himself was voted Yugoslavia's best player of the qualifiers.

His performances for Lazio have played a major part this past season in their remarkable start both in Serie A and the Champions League in which he was quickly on goal-scoring target with his free kicks. Such was his impact that there was a media campaign in Italy to put his name forward as a candidate for European Footballer of the Year.

Regardless of international acclaim, Mihajlovic is proud of his popular reputation in his home country. As he says, "People are even saying that they should give me a diplomatic passport or make me some sort of goodwill ambassador for my country." Mihajlovic, who already knows how it feels to be a European champion after his Champions Cup triumph with Red Star Belgrade in 1991, certainly has the international profile.

"Mihajlovic has such ability with free kicks, for a defender, that it's like having twelve players in your team"

Sven-Goran Eriksson
Lazio coach

Peter Schmeichel

Denmark

One of the best compliments to Peter Schmeichel is the trouble Manchester United have had in trying to replace him. He decided that he would quit English football at the end of the 1998–99 season, taking an amazing 10 winners' medals away with him.

In his time with United Schmeichel won all that Europe had to offer, including two domestic doubles, the treble and the UEFA European Football Championship™ with Denmark in 1992. In his last three games for United, he won the League, the FA Cup and the European Champions League, where he had the honour of receiving the Cup as stand-in captain for the suspended Roy Keane. He is also one of only three goal-keepers in England to have won three FA Cup winners' medals.

However, Schmeichel maintains that the highlight of his career is Denmark's victory in 1992. He likens the triumph of such a tiny nation to Wimbledon winning the FA Cup – "The final was the match of my life and nothing can beat Euro 92."

It was at the UEFA European Football Championship™ of 1988 that Schmeichel first rose to international prominence, replacing Troels Rasmussen in Denmark's final match.

All this success is a long way from his humble beginnings in part-time Danish soccer. He had to take on various other jobs, including running a shop for the World Wildlife Fund and working as a newspaper advertising salesman, before moving from Brondby to Manchester. United manager Sir Alex Ferguson has nothing but praise for Schmeichel and all

this for the now paltry sum of £750,000 in 1991.

There had been talk of Schmeichel going back to Denmark after quitting United, but he wanted to sample life in another country before returning to his homeland. With clubs all over Europe queueing for his signature, he chose Sporting Lisbon where he is helping them rekindle their challenge at the head of the Portuguese top division.

His passion for the game is evident every time he plays. He is renowned for the force of his instructions to his defence. Indeed, he has proved a commanding presence in both penalty areas, often having been seen dashing up for United corners late in the game and even scoring in a European tie. More of that would make European history!

"He's the best goalkeeper I've ever been involved with in the game"

Sir Alex Ferguson, Manchester United manager

Schmeichel: 1992 champion.

★ FACTFILE ★

Position	: Goalkeeper
Club	: Sporting (Portugal)
Previous clubs	: Hvidovre, Brondby, Manchester United (England)
Born	: 18 November 1963
Intl apps	: 117
Intl goals	: 0

David Beckham

England

David Beckham has provided the perfect answer to all those who questioned whether he would survive the fall-out from his disastrous sending-off at the 1998 FIFA World Cup finals. He simply got on with his football and played a leading role in Manchester United's treble-winning season.

Beckham: new generation

All in all, 1999 was a remarkable year for Beckham. In addition to the treble, he married Spice Girl Victoria Adams, with whom he now has a son, Brooklyn. He could also add a World Club Cup medal to his growing collection.

Beckham is a lifelong United fan. As a boy he dreamed of playing for the Red Devils; there was never any other team in the reckoning, despite offers from local clubs in London. Since signing for United as a schoolboy in 1991, he has risen through the junior ranks, winning an FA Youth Cup medal, through the England Under-21s to become a regular with both club and country. In 1997 he won the PFA Young Player of the Year award.

He is renowned for having one of the best crosses in the game, with a ferocious shot, potent at free kicks. Most famously, he scored a wonderful goal from the halfway line against Wimbledon at the start of his first full season as a United regular.

It will be interesting to see whether England use him in EURO 2000™ at wide right, where his crossing ability will be most useful, or in what is apparently his preferred position in central midfield. For most of his time at United he has performed solidly on the right, providing the service which has helped establish Dwight Yorke and Andy Cole as one of the most prolific strike forces in the Premiership. However, in both last year's UEFA Champions League and FA Cup finals he played in the centre and, despite some critics saying he dropped a little too deep, worked effectively in controlling the play.

Manager Kevin Keegan and Beckham himself readily admit he has not yet performed at his best for England, though that could be said about many of the England squad. Keegan sees the problem as being one of comfort and confidence. He believes that once Beckham finds a set position in a settled side he will offer the performances that have helped United achieve the European glory England would love to emulate.

"Beckham is a great player. I can't think of anyone else who provides so many assists for goals"

Rivaldo, European Footballer of the Year, Barcelona 1999

 FACTFILE

Position	: Midfield
Club	: Manchester United
Previous clubs	: Preston (on loan)
Born	: 2 May 1975
Intl apps	: 27
Intl goals	: 1

Alan Shearer
England

Alan Shearer's revival under Bobby Robson at Newcastle has come at just the right time for him to lead England into EURO 2000™.

After a personally successful Euro 96, when he scored four goals in the group stages and the semi-final goal against Germany, Shearer's international form, like much of the England team's, has been patchy. His domestic form suffered from the revolving door manager's position at Newcastle, plus the combined pressures of leading a struggling team and the increasing animosity of opposition supporters.

In France 98, Shearer scored the all-important first goal against Tunisia, and a nerveless penalty against Argentina. Those who question his continued ability at the top level would do well to remember his performances when it really counts. This is where Shearer's experience and strength show through. While now a senior pro, particularly in comparison with youngsters such as Michael Owen, Emile Heskey and Robbie Fowler, Shearer's finishing and power to lead make him an almost automatic first choice.

Shearer had wanted to start his professional career with Newcastle – he also tried out as a goalkeeper for them – but they let him slip through their fingers. It was to prove a costly mistake. Ever since his professional debut, scoring a hat-trick for Southampton in a 4–2 victory over Arsenal, Shearer has proved himself a natural goalscorer. In fact, he is the highest goalscorer in the Premiership's eight-year history.

In the first of his record-breaking transfers he moved from Southampton to Blackburn Rovers for £3.3 million. It was at Blackburn that he established the formidable SAS partnership with Chris Sutton, a partnership that yielded 49 goals (of which Shearer scored 34 – easily top scorer for the season).

A bold move by Newcastle manager Kevin Keegan in 1996 brought Shearer to Tyneside for another record fee, this time a then world record £15 million. He has been one of the only ever-presents throughout the troubled reigns of Dalglish and Gullit.

Shearer is rightly regarded as England's best forward of the decade. He scored on his debuts for Southampton, Blackburn and England. He is the only player to have scored more than 30 goals in a Premiership season and, even when not scoring himself, he works the defenders and drags them out creating space for others. It's an ideal combination for a centre-forward and captain.

Shearer: high-scoring skipper.

FACTFILE

Position	: **Centre-forward**
Club	: **Newcastle United**
Previous clubs	: **Southampton, Blackburn Rovers**
Born	: **13 August 1970**
Intl apps	: **56**
Intl goals	: **28**

"At his best there is no centre-forward to compare with him anywhere in Europe, and I should know"

Bobby Robson
Newcastle manager

Zlatko Zahovic

Slovenia

Slovenia surprised many by qualifying at the expense of the Ukraine in the EURO 2000™ play-offs. Olympiakos forward Zlatko Zahovic provided their first goal in the first leg to set them on their way to their first-ever international finals.

Zahovic's performances in Slovenia's qualifying for EURO 2000™, combined with an excellent season for then club Porto, earned him the 1998–99 Slovene Player of the Year award. Including the all-important play-off, Zahovic scored an amazing eight goals to spearhead Slovenia's charge. If he could manage just half that total in the tournament itself, Slovenia could spring more surprises.

His speed and movement in and around the penalty area combine with a confident left foot to make many in his homeland regard him as the greatest talent to come out of Slovenia since Yugoslav 1974 FIFA World Cup star Branko Oblak.

Interestingly, Zahovic has never played in the Slovenian domestic league. At the age of 16 he went to Partizan Belgrade, where he played alongside Yugoslav star Pedrag Mijatovic. In 1993 he picked up a Yugoslav league championship winner's medal. That summer he went to Portugal with Vitoria Guimaraes before moving on to the mighty Porto in 1997. Zahovic helped Porto to extend their run in the league to a record five successive championships, winning the title in both seasons he was there.

In his second season, 1998–99, he was top scorer in the Champions League after the group stage. Despite the fact that Zahovic scored an impressive seven goals in six games, it was not enough to take Porto through to the quarter-finals.

In this same season he forged a devastating partnership with Brazilian Mario Jardel. These two scored 50 goals between them, whilst Porto as a whole scored a massive 85 – more than 20 goals better than the next highest-scoring team.

Having scored against them in both the home and away games in the Champions League in the previous season, Zahovic moved to Greek champions Olympiakos in the summer of 1999.

Zahovic will be using EURO 2000™ as his chance to join old team-mate Mijatovic in the world-class bracket.

> **"I take a lot of credit for my goals which Zahovic really deserves because of the way he opens up defences"**
>
> Mario Jardel
> former FC Porto team-mate

Zahovic: prodigal son.

★ FACTFILE ★

Position	: Forward
Club	: Olympiakos (Greece)
Previous clubs	: Partizan Belgrade (Yugoslavia), Vitoria Guimaraes (Portugal), FC Porto (Portugal)
Born	: 1 February 1971
Intl apps	: 40
Intl goals	: 19

Hakan Sukur

Turkey

Centre-forward Hakan Sukur has been a Galatasaray fan since his childhood, and it is there he feels most at home. Going abroad is not something that Hakan handles very well. In the summer of 1995 he was tempted by the bright lights of Italy's *Serie A* and joined Torino for £3 million.

Five months later Galatasaray were paying Torino their money back and bringing Hakan home. He never overcame his homesickness, saying, "It was hard being so far away from Galatasaray. I was a fan of the club from childhood. It's hard when you go to a new country and don't understand the language. I spent hours each evening on the phone."

In England for Euro 96 Hakan had not recovered from this unhappy spell. Turkey had not qualified for a major tournament for 42 years and their lack of international experience showed. They had a disappointing time of it, ending the tournament bottom of their group, the only team not to score a single goal.

Back with his first love the next season, however, Hakan set about restoring the belief expressed by Nedo Sonetti, the man who took him to Torino. Since returning to Turkey, he has been league top scorer three seasons running, twice scoring more than 30 goals.

Hakan was destined for sport from an early age. A promising basketball player, he was swayed towards football by his father who played for hometown club

Hakan: beating a jinx.

Sakarya in the second and third divisions before becoming general manager. Hakan joined their junior section aged seven. He made his senior debut for Sakaryaspor at 16, moving to Bursapor at 18, before his boyhood dream came true, and Galatasaray bought him in 1991 to replace the legendary Tanju Colak.

Hakan's goals have been instrumental in Turkey's qualifying, most memorably the one that beat Germany in Bursa, as the European champions were pushed to hold on to top spot in their group. He will hope to break his awayday jinx and prove he is a true great, building on Turkey's growing pride in its national side.

★ FACTFILE ★

Position	: Centre-forward
Club	: Galatasaray
Previous clubs	: Sakaryaspor, Bursaspor, Galatasaray, Torino (Italy)
Born	: 1 September 1971
Intl apps	: 50
Intl goals	: 26

"Hakan Sukur, without any doubt, has all the qualities needed to become a truly great player"

Nedo Sonetti
former Torino coach

A Glorious Past

Frenchman Henri Delaunay was the "father" of the European Championship, a concept which was first proposed to the world governing body, FIFA, as far back as 5 February 1927. However, priority was given to the creation of the FIFA World Cup and Delaunay's idea had to wait until after the European federation, UEFA, was set up in 1954. Delaunay became the general secretary and was thus in an ideal position to turn his dream into reality. Unfortunately he died before the launch of the initial event in 1959–60 but it was deemed fitting that the prize for which 50 nations across the continent now compete every four years should bear his name – the Henri Delaunay Trophy.

Delaunay: founding father.

The first championship drew a cautious response from the nations of Europe – just 17 entered. Italy, West Germany – both future champions – and England were among the absentees. France, appropriately, staged the finals. Four nations were involved, playing knock-out semi-finals, a third-place play-off and a final. The Soviet Union, including legendary goalkeeper Lev Yashin, thrashed Czechoslovakia 3–0 in Marseille in one semi-final, while hosts France lost a Paris thriller 5–4 against Yugoslavia in the other, despite leading 4–2 with 15 minutes left.

The final was played in the old Parc des Princes, just as the first Champion Clubs Cup Final had been four years earlier. The first goal was almost an own goal, Soviet skipper Igor Netto deflecting a strike from Milan Galic, who was credited with the goal. But right-wing Slava Metrevelli equalized and centre-forward Viktor Ponedelnik claimed an extra-time winner.

The Soviet holders were favourites to retain the trophy in the second tournament in 1964. England competed for the first time but were eliminated in the qualifying rounds. Alf Ramsey's first competitive experience at national team level ended in 2–5 and 1–1 defeats by a French team inspired by veteran Raymond Kopa.

In the quarter-finals Spain beat the Irish Republic 7–1 on aggregate and the Soviet Union defeated Sweden. The Soviets had previously beaten a reviving Italy thanks to a penalty save by Yashin from Sandro Mazzola.

Denmark and Hungary also qualified for the finals in Spain. The Danes were well

1960
Lev Yashin

The greatest hero of Soviet soccer was legendary goalkeeper Yashin who played more than 100 times for his country and remains the only goalkeeper to have won the European Footballer of the Year trophy. Yashin, who played all his career with Moscow Dynamo, produced decisive saves against Yugoslavia in the final.

Lev Yashin: hero of the Soviet Union.

beaten 3–0 by the Soviet Union in their Barcelona semi-final, and Spain, leaning on the midfield inspiration of Luis Suarez and the right-wing magic of Amancio, defeated Hungary 2–1 in Madrid. Spain took an early lead in the final in Madrid through Jesus Pereda. Khusainov struck back for the Soviet Union but a second-half strike from Zaragoza centre-forward Marcelino was the signal for Spanish celebrations.

Four years later in 1968, for the second successive tournament, the hosts – this time Italy – ended up as champions. The dramatic success of the 1964 event was reflected in an increased entry for 1968 and UEFA thus converted the qualifying competition from the direct elimination system into a mini-league formula. Italy earned the right to stage the finals not through seeding but thanks to a qualifying campaign in which the team, under the managership of Ferruccio Valcareggi, overcame Cyprus, Switzerland and Romania in the group round, then Bulgaria in the direct elimination quarter-finals. The other finalists were Yugoslavia and the Soviet Union as well as FIFA World Cup-holders England. Italy included great figures such as goalkeeper Dino Zoff, left-back Giacinto Facchetti and attackers Pietro Anastasi and Luigi Riva, but they still needed some luck. The toss of a coin earned them a place in the final after their semi-final against the Soviet Union finished goalless following extra time. The penalty shoot-out had yet to be introduced into top-level competition.

In the other semi-final Yugoslavia won 1–0 in Florence in a match which was doubly disappointing for England, who were making their finals debut. Alan Mullery became the first England player to be sent off while representing his country in a senior international. Yugoslavia, inspired by the left-wing skills of Dragan Dzajic, were favoured to beat Italy in the final in Rome. Dzajic provided the Slavs with an early lead but Angelo Domenghini equalized controversially from a free kick with 10 minutes remaining. Extra time failed to provide any more goals so the final went to a replay in Florence. This time Yugoslavia were too tired to resist the thrusts of Riva and Anastasi. Italy were European champions for the first – and, so far, only – time.

Italy's attempt to retain the crown in 1972 was brought to an abrupt end in the quarter-finals by Belgium, who then won the vote to host the finals. The most outstanding side in the competition was West Germany whose manager, Helmut Schön, had built a new team on a nucleus provided by Bayern Munich and Borussia Münchengladbach defeated Hungary in Brussels to reach their third final in four competitions. In the other semi-final Belgium lost 2–1 to West Germany.

Franz Beckenbauer and his team were clear favourites to win the final in the Heysel Stadium in Brussels. The Soviet Union never threatened. Netzer dominated midfield and hit a post before two typically opportunist strikes from Müller and another from Herbert Wimmer decided the match. The 3–0 scoreline remains the largest winning margin of any UEFA European Football Championship™ final.

Spain's midfield general was another European Footballer of the Year and arguably the greatest player Spain has ever produced.

1964
Luis Suarez

He started with La Coruña, made his name with Barcelona then earned World and European Cup-winning glory after transferring for a world record £210,000 to Inter Milan.

Italy has a tradition of great goalkeepers and none have been greater than Zoff who defied the Soviet Union and Yugoslavia in the 1968 finals.

1968
Dino Zoff

Zoff won an Italian record of 112 international caps and captained his country to victory in the 1982 FIFA World Cup. He won just about every club prize with Juventus.

West Germany's captain dictated his team's performances from a revolutionary role as attacking sweeper, or libero.

1972
Franz Beckenbauer

Bayern Munich's captain later made history as the only man to captain and then manage his country to FIFA World Cup sucess. Beckenbauer won 103 international caps, a record at the time.

Franz Beckenbauer: skipper, sweeper, playmaker.

But if the 1972 finals had produced an outstanding team in West Germany, the 1976 event went three better by producing no fewer than four superbly competitive sides. Hosts Yugoslavia finished fourth after losing the third-place play-off to Holland, but there could be no embarrassment in that. These stand as probably the most thrilling finals of the first generation of the tournament, with the final between Czechoslovakia and holders West Germany a dramatic classic.

The Germans had found a new Müller – Dieter Müller from Köln. He scored a hat-trick in the semi-final against Yugoslavia and led the German fight-back in the final after they had gone 2–0 down in 25 minutes. One minute remained of normal time when Bernd Holzenbein's equalizer sent the game into extra time. No more goals came and Czechoslovakia duly won the first major event decided on a penalty shoot-out when playmaker Antonin Panenka sent goalkeeper Sepp Maier the wrong way with the decisive kick.

It turned out to be the end of an era. By 1980, such was the popularity of the tournament and the pressure for places, that UEFA decided to increase the scope of the finals to take in eight countries. They were split into two groups of four with the group-winners meeting in the final. Italy became the first nation to host the finals twice. They finished runners-up in their group behind Belgium and ahead of England and Spain. In the other group old rivals West Germany finished ahead of Holland, title-holders Czechoslovakia and newcomers Greece.

A 48,000 crowd, well below capacity, turned out for the final in Rome. A new German hero emerged in that game, Bayern Munich's Karl-Heinz Rummenigge. He contributed the inch-perfect corner from which giant Horst Hrubesch headed a last-minute winning goal to beat the Belgians.

In 1984 France drove a coach and horses through the myth that host nations only succeed because of inordinately unfair advantages. After going close to winning the 1982 FIFA World Cup, this magnificent French side was unarguably the cream of the continent in the early 1980s, and they swept all before them to win the ultimate prize against Spain in the new Parc des Princes stadium in Paris. The changing balance of the international game was reflected in these finals. France's brilliance emanated from the midfield trio of hard-working Luis Fernandez and Jean Tigana, plus effervescent little Alain Giresse, topped off by the all-round attacking genius of Michel Platini.

France beat Spain 2–0 in the final. Injuries and suspensions wrecked the Spanish tactical plan, but it was an uncharacteristic slip by goalkeeper-captain Luis Arconada after 56 minutes –

Rummenigge was a raw youngster when Bayern Munich lifted him into their European Cup-winning side in the mid 1970s.

1980
Karl-Heinz
Rummenigge

He learned his lessons from Beckenbauer and Gerd Müller so well that he proved to be West Germany's European inspiration in Italy and earned himself a lucrative transfer to Inter Milan.

Viktor starred in goal for the dominant Czechoslovak army club, Dukla Prague.

1976
Ivo Viktor

His defensive colleagues took their orders from him to enormous effect. The Czechoslovaks went into the finals as outsiders but Viktor's secure handling inspired their victories over Holland and West Germany

Michel Platini: a captain who led by example.

Hat-trick hero: Marco Van Basten takes England apart in 1988.

allowing Platini's low drive from a free kick to spin through his grasp – which proved to be the decisive blow. France overcame the sending-off of Le Roux after 84 minutes and Bruno Bellone scored a second in the final minute, but their lead had never been seriously threatened.

France were not the only nation for whom UEFA European Football Championship™ success had proved elusive. The same could be said of Holland, FIFA World Cup runners-up in 1974 and 1978. But in 1988 they finally secured the major prize which their pre-eminence in the international game had long since demanded.

Marco Van Basten was the Dutch hero, scoring a hat-trick against England in the group matches and a wonderful, volleyed goal against the Soviet Union in the final. Skipper Ruud Gullit scored the first goal and keeper Hans Van Breukelen saved a penalty from Igor Belanov to defy the Soviets just when it seemed they might be coming back into the game.

Denmark came from nowhere to win the tournament in 1992 in Sweden. Political upheavals across the continent caused major disruption from the start of the qualifying groups. The former East Germany was consigned to history just as the qualifying tournament began and the GDR federation, as one of its last acts, withdrew from the event. This allowed key players, such as midfielder Matthias Sammer and forwards Thomas Doll and Andreas Thom, to play for a unified Germany in the finals.

As for Yugoslavia, they had been one of the more outstanding qualifiers but in the spring of 1992 the country was engulfed in internal conflict. UEFA barred them from the finals on security grounds and recalled Denmark – runners-up in the Slavs' qualifying group – in their stead and at two weeks' notice.

Van Basten was Holland's greatest player after his friend and mentor Johan Cruyff.

1988
Marco
Van Basten

In the 1988 finals, he scored a magnificent first-round hat-trick against England and a wonderful, decisive goal against the Soviet Union in the final. Sadly, Van Basten was later forced to retire prematurely by injury.

France's playmaker and driving force was also their nine-goal top scorer.

1984
Michel Platini

He scored against Denmark and fired hat-tricks against Belgium and Yugoslavia in the group games, scored against Portugal in the semi-finals and then scored the first goal in the final against Spain, before lifting the trophy in his extra role as national captain. Platini was three times European Footballer of the Year.

Shock success: Denmark celebrate their amazing victory in 1992 in Gothenburg.

Denmark's massive goal-keeper was one of their heroes in the most unlikely Euro win of them all.

1992
Peter Schmeichel

In the semi-final he defied all Holland's efforts and psyched Van Basten into the decisive miss in the penalty shoot-out. Schmeichel went on to further glory at club level with Manchester United.

Denmark were runners-up in their first-round group behind Sweden but they beat Holland on penalties in the semi-final and, incredibly, Germany in the final. Berti Vogts's men had been clear favourites but the Danes – from manager Richard Moller Nielsen to goalkeeper Peter Schmeichel, skipper Lars Olsen, midfielder Kim Vilfort and forward Brian Laudrup – had not read the script. Goals from John Jensen and Vilfort duly produced one of the greatest shocks in the competition's history.

By now, the UEFA European Football Championship™ was well established as the top national team event after the FIFA World Cup itself. Pressure to reach the finals was growing more intense all the time. UEFA thus enlarged the event in 1996, in England, to 16 nations.

The tournament was a massive success, a major public relations triumph for the game in general and England in particular. The only regret England took from the tournament was that Terry Venables' team did not win the event for the first time. Instead England were victims of an old jinx – a semi-final penalty shoot-out loss, to Germany.

The Germans went on to secure a record third UEFA European Football Championship™ success and did so by taking advantage of the controversial new golden-goal rule in the final against the Czech Republic. The score was 1–1 when substitute striker Oliver Bierhoff scored the event-stopping winner four minutes into extra time at Wembley. It was the first time a major senior tournament had been settled by this method.

Golden goal: Oliver Bierhoff's Euro 96 winner.

Sammer used his pace, vision and skill to control Germany's performances from a nominal role as sweeper.

1996
Matthias Sammer

His cool head proved vital as the tournament went on and injury-hit Germany had to hit back from a goal down against England in the semi-final and the Czech Republic in the final.

Previous Finals

1960 France

SEMI-FINALS
Yugoslavia 5 *(Galic 11, Zanetic 55, Knez 75, Jerkovic 77, 79)*
France 4 *(Vincent 12, Heutte 43, 62, Wisnieski 52)*

Soviet Union 3 *(V. Ivanov 35, 58, Ponedelnik 64)*
Czechoslovakia 0

THIRD PLACE PLAY-OFF
Czechoslovakia 2 *(Bubernik 58, Pavlovic 88)* France 0

FINAL, 10 July, Parc des Princes, Paris
Soviet Union 2 *(Metrevelli 49, Ponedelnik 113)*
Yugoslavia 1 *(Galic 41)* after extra time
HALF-TIME: 0–1 • 90 MINUTES: 1–1 • ATT: 17,966 • REF: Ellis (England)
Soviet Union: *Yashin, Chekheli, Maslenkin, Krutikov, Voinov, Netto, Metrevelli, V. Ivanov, Ponedelnik, Bubukhin, Meshki.*
Yugoslavia: *Vidinic, Durkovic, Miladinovic, Jusufi, Zanetic, Perusic, Matus, Jerkovic, Galic, Sekularac, Kostic.*

1964 Spain

SEMI-FINALS
Spain 2 *(Pereda 35, Amancio 115)* Hungary 1 *(Bene 85)*
after extra time

Soviet Union 3 *(Voronin 19, Ponedelnik 40, V. Ivanov 88)*
Denmark 0

THIRD PLACE PLAY-OFF
Hungary 3 *(Bene 11, Novak 107 pen, 110)* Denmark 1
(Bertelsen 81) after extra time

FINAL, 21 June, Santiago Bernabeu, Madrid
Spain 2 *(Pereda 6, Marcelino 83)* Soviet Union 1 *(Khusainov 8)*
HALF-TIME: 1–1 • ATT: 125,000 • REF: Holland (England)
Spain: *Iribar, Rivilla, Olivella, Calleja, Zoco, Fuste, Amancio, Pereda, Marcelino, Suarez, Lapetra.*
Soviet Union: *Yashin, Shustikov, Shesternev, Mudrik, Voronin, Anichkin, Chislenko, V. Ivanov, Ponedelnik, Korneyev, Khusainov.*

1968 Italy

SEMI-FINALS
Yugoslavia 1 *(Dzajic 85)* England 0

Italy 0 Soviet Union 0 Italy on toss of a coin after extra time

THIRD PLACE PLAY-OFF
England 2 *(Charlton 39, Hurst 63)* Soviet Union 0

FINAL, 8 June, Olimpico, Rome
Italy 1 *(Domenghini 80)* Yugoslavia 1 *(Dzajic 38)* after extra time
HALF-TIME: 0–1 • 90 MINUTES: 1–1 • ATT: 85,000
• REF: Dienst (Switzerland)
Italy: *Zoff, Castano, Burgnich, Guarneri, Facchetti, Ferrini, Juliano, Lodetti, Domenghini, Anastasi, Prati.*
Yugoslavia: *Pantelic, Fazlagic, Holcer, Paunovic, Damjanovic, Acimovic, Trivic, Pavlovic, Petkovic, Musemic, Dzajic.*

REPLAY, 10 June, Comunale, Florence
Italy 2 *(Riva 12, Anastasi 31)* Yugoslavia 0
HALF-TIME: 2–0 • ATT: 50,000 • REF: Ortiz de Mendibil (Spain)
Italy: *Zoff, Salvadore, Burgnich, Guarneri, Facchetti, Rosato, De Sisti, Domenghini, Mazzola, Anastasi, Riva.*
Yugoslavia: *Pantelic, Fazlagic, Paunovic, Holcer, Damjanovic, Acimovic, Trivic, Pavlovic, Hosic, Musemic, Dzajic.*

1972 Belgium

SEMI-FINALS
Soviet Union 1 *(Konkov 53)* Hungary 0

West Germany 2 *(G. Müller 24, 72)* Belgium 1 *(Polleunis 83)*

THIRD PLACE PLAY-OFF
Belgium 2 *(Lambert 24, Van Himst 28)* Hungary 1 *(Ku 53 pen)*

FINAL, 18 June, Heysel, Brussels
West Germany 3 *(G. Müller 27, 57, Wimmer 52)* Soviet Union 0
HALF-TIME: 1–0 • ATT: 50,000 • REF: Marschall (Austria)
West Germany: *Maier, Hottges, Beckenbauer, Schwarzenbeck, Breitner, Hoeness, Netzer, Wimmer, Heynckes, G. Müller, E. Kremers.*
Soviet Union: *Rudakov, Dzodzuashvili, Khurtsilava, Kaplichni, Istomin, Kolotov, Troshkin, Konkov (Dolmatov 46), Baidachni, Banishevski (Kozenkevich 65), Onishenko.*

1976 Yugoslavia

SEMI-FINALS
Czechoslovakia 3 *(Ondrus 20, Nehoda 115, F. Vesely 118)*
Holland 1 *(Ondrus og 74)* after extra time

West Germany 4 *(Flohe 65, D. Müller 80, 114, 119)*
Yugoslavia 2 *(Popivoda 20, Djazic 30)* after extra time

THIRD PLACE PLAY-OFF
Holland 3 *(Geels 27, 106, W. van de Kerkhof 39)*
Yugoslavia 2 *(Katalinski 43, Dzajic 82)* after extra time

FINAL, 20 June, Crvena Zvezda (Red Star), Belgrade
Czechoslovakia 2 *(Svehlik 8, Dobias 25)*
West Germany 2 *(D. Müller 28, Holzenbein 89)*
Czechoslovakia 5–3 on pens, after extra time
HALF-TIME: 2–1 • 90 MINUTES: 2–2 • ATT: 33,000 • REF: Gonella (Italy)
Czechoslovakia: *Viktor, Pivarnik, Ondrus, Capkovic, Gogh, Dobias, Panenka, Moder, Masny, Svehlik (Jurkemik 79), Nehoda.*
West Germany: *Maier, Vogts, Beckenbauer, Schwarzenbeck, Dietz, Wimmer (Flohe 46), Bonhof, Beer (Bongartz 79), Hoeness, D. Müller, Holzenbein.*

1980 Italy

GROUP 1
West Germany 1 *(Rummenigge 55)* Czechoslovakia 0

Holland 1 *(Kist 56 pen)* Greece 0

West Germany 3 *(K. Allofs 15, 60, 68)*
Holland 2 *(Rep 75 pen, W. van der Kerkhof 86)*

Czechoslovakia 3 *(Panenka 5, Vizek 25, Nehoda 63)*
Greece 1 *(Anastopoulos 11)*

Czechoslovakia 1 *(Nehoda 13)* Holland 1 *(Kist 58)*

West Germany 0 Greece 0

	P	W	D	L	F	A	Pts
West Germany	3	2	1	0	4	2	5
Czechoslovakia	3	1	1	1	4	3	3
Holland	3	1	1	1	4	4	3
Greece	3	0	1	2	1	4	1

GROUP 2
England 1 *(Wilkins 32)* Belgium 1 *(Ceulemans 38)*

Italy 0 Spain 0

Belgium 2 *(Gerets 17, Cools 64)* **Spain 1** *(Quini 35)*

Italy 1 *(Tardelli 78)* **England 0**

England 2 *(Brooking 18, Woodcock 62)* **Spain 1** *(Dani 48 pen)*

Italy 0 Belgium 0

	P	W	D	L	F	A	Pts
Belgium	3	1	2	0	3	2	4
Italy	3	1	2	0	1	0	4
England	3	1	1	1	3	3	3
Spain	3	0	1	2	2	4	1

THIRD PLACE PLAY-OFF
Czechoslovakia 1 *(Jurkemik 48)* • **Italy 1** *(Graziani 74)*
Czechoslovakia 9-8 on pens, after extra time

FINAL, 22 June, Olimpico, Rome
West Germany 2 *(Hrubesch 10, 88)* **Belgium 1** *(Vandereycken 71 pen)*
HALF-TIME: 1–0 • ATT: 48,000 • REF: Rainea (Romania)
West Germany: *Schumacher, Kaltz, Stielike, K. Forster, Dietz, Briegel (Cullmann 55), Schuster, H. Müller, Rummenigge, Hrubesch, K. Allofs.*
Belgium: *Pfaff, Gerets, L. Millecamps, Meeuws, Renquin, Cools, Vandereycken, Van Moer, Mommens, François van der Elst, Ceulemans.*

1984 France
GROUP 1
France 1 *(Platini 77)* **Denmark 0**

Belgium 2 *(Vandenbergh 27, Grun 44)* **Yugoslavia 0**

France 5 *(Platini 3, 74, 88, Giresse 32, Fernandez 43)* **Belgium 0**

Denmark 5 *(Ivkovic og 7, Berggren 16, Arnesen 68, Elkjaer 81, Lauridsen 83)* **Yugoslavia 0**

France 3 *(Platini 59, 61, 76)* **Yugoslavia 2** *(Sestic 31, Stojkovic 80)*

Denmark 3 *(Arnesen 40, Brylle 60, Elkjaer 83)*
Belgium 2 *(Ceulemans 25, Vercauteren 38)*

	P	W	D	L	F	A	Pts
France	3	3	0	0	9	2	6
Denmark	3	2	0	1	8	3	4
Belgium	3	1	0	2	4	8	2
Yugoslavia	3	0	0	3	2	10	0

GROUP 2
West Germany 0 Portugal 0

Spain 1 *(Carrasco 20)* **Romania 1** *(Boloni 34)*

West Germany 2 *(Völler 24, 65)* **Romania 1** *(Coras 46)*

Portugal 1 *(Sousa 51)* **Spain 1** *(Santillana 72)*

Spain 1 *(Maceda 89)* **West Germany 0**

Portugal 1 *(Nene 80)* **Romania 0**

	P	W	D	L	F	A	Pts
Spain	3	1	2	0	3	2	4
Portugal	3	1	2	0	2	1	4
West Germany	3	1	1	1	2	2	3
Romania	3	0	1	2	2	4	1

SEMI-FINALS
France 3 *(Domergue 24, 114, Platini 119)* **Portugal 2** *(Jordao 73, 97)* after extra time

Spain 1 *(Maceda 66)* **Denmark 1** *(Lerby 6)*
Spain 5–4 on pens, after extra time

FINAL, 27 June, Parc des Princes, Paris
France 2 *(Platini 56, Bellone 90)* **Spain 0**
HALF-TIME: 0–0 • ATT: 47,368 • REF: Christov (Czechoslovakia)
France: *Bats, Battiston (Amoros 72), *Le Roux, Bossis, Domergue, Fernandez, Giresse, Tigana, Platini, Lacombe (Genghini 79), Bellone. *Le Roux sent off, 84 minutes.*
Spain: *Arconada, Urquiaga, Salva (Roberto 84), Gallego, Senor, Francisco, Victor, Camacho, Julio Alberto (Sarabia 76), Santillana, Carrasco.*

1988 West Germany
GROUP 1
West Germany 1 *(Brehme 55)* **Italy 1** *(Mancini 51)*

Spain 3 *(Michel 5, Butragueño 52, Gordillo 67)*
Denmark 2 *(M. Laudrup 25, Povlsen 85)*

West Germany 2 *(Klinsmann 9, Thon 85)* **Denmark 0**

Italy 1 *(Vialli 73)* **Spain 0**

West Germany 2 *(Völler 30, 51)* **Spain 0**

Italy 2 *(Altobelli 65, De Agostini 87)* **Denmark 0**

	P	W	D	L	F	A	Pts
West Germany	3	2	1	0	5	1	5
Italy	3	2	1	0	4	1	5
Spain	3	1	0	2	3	5	2
Denmark	3	0	0	3	2	7	0

GROUP 2
Republic of Ireland 1 *(Houghton 5)* **England 0**

Soviet Union 1 *(Rats 53)* **Holland 0**

Holland 3 *(Van Basten 23, 71, 75)* **England 1** *(Robson 53)*

Soviet Union 1 *(Protasov 75)* **Republic of Ireland 1** *(Whelan 38)*

Soviet Union 3 *(Aleinikov 3, Mikhailichenko 28, Pasulko 72)*
England 1 *(Adams 16)*

Holland 1 *(Kieft 82)* **Republic of Ireland 0**

	P	W	D	L	F	A	Pts
Soviet Union	3	2	1	0	5	2	5
Holland	3	2	0	1	4	2	4
Republic of Ireland	3	1	1	1	2	2	3
England	3	0	0	3	2	7	0

SEMI-FINALS
Holland 2 *(R. Koeman 73 pen, Van Basten 88)*
West Germany 1 *(Matthäus 54 pen)*

Soviet Union 2 *(Litovchenko 59, Protasov 62)* **Italy 0**

FINAL, 25 June, Olympiastadion, Munich
Holland 2 *(Gullit 33, Van Basten 54)* **Soviet Union 0**
HALF-TIME: 1–0 • ATT: 72,300 • REF: Vautrot (France)
Holland: *Van Breukelen, Van Aerle, R. Koeman, Rijkaard, Van Tiggelen, Vanenburg, Wouters, E. Koeman, Muhren, Gullit, Van Basten.*
Soviet Union: *Dasayev, Khidiatulin, Demianenko, Litovchenko, Aleinikov, Zavarov, Belanov, Mikhailichenko, Gotsmanov (Baltacha 69), Rats, Protasov (Pasulko 71).*

1992 Sweden
GROUP A
Sweden 1 *(Eriksson 26)* **France 1** *(Papin 59)*

Denmark 0 England 0

France 0 England 0

Sweden 1 *(Brolin 58)* Denmark 0

Denmark 2 *(Larsen 7, Elstrup 78)* France 1 *(Papin 58)*

Sweden 2 *(Eriksson 51, Brolin 84)* England 1 *(Platt 3)*

	P	W	D	L	F	A	Pts
Sweden	3	2	1	0	4	2	5
Denmark	3	1	1	1	2	2	3
France	3	0	2	1	2	3	2
England	3	0	2	1	1	2	2

GROUP B

Holland 1 *(Bergkamp 7)* Scotland 0

Germany 1 *(Hässler 90)* CIS 1 *(Dobrovolski 63)*

Germany 2 *(Riedle 29, Effenberg 47)* Scotland 0

Holland 0 CIS 0

Holland 3 *(Rijkaard 3, Rob Witschge 15, Bergkamp 73)*
Germany 1 *(Klinsmann 53)*

Scotland 3 *(McStay 6, McClair 17, McAllister 83 pen)* CIS 0

	P	W	D	L	F	A	Pts
Holland	3	2	1	0	4	1	5
Germany	3	1	1	1	4	4	3
Scotland	3	1	0	2	3	3	2
CIS	3	0	2	1	1	4	2

SEMI-FINALS

Germany 3 *(Hässler 11, Riedle 59, 88)*
Sweden 2 *(Brolin 64, Andersson 89)*

Denmark 2 *(H. Larsen 5, 32)* Holland 2 *(Bergkamp 23, Rijkaard 85)* Denmark 5–4 on pens, after extra time

FINAL, 26 June, Nya Ullevi, Gothenburg
Denmark 2 *(Jensen 18, Vilfort 78)* Germany 0
HALF-TIME: 1–0 • ATT: 37,000 • REF: Galler (Switzerland)
Denmark: *Schmeichel, Sivebaek (Christiansen 66), K. Nielsen, L. Olsen, Piechnik, Christofte, Vilfort, J. Jensen, H. Larsen, B. Laudrup, Povlsen.*
Germany: *Illgner, Reuter, Kohler, Helmer, Brehme, Buchwald, Effenberg (Thom 80), Sammer (Doll 46), Hässler, Klinsmann, Riedle.*

1996 England

GROUP A

England 1 *(Shearer 23)* Switzerland 1 *(Turkyilmaz 82 pen)*

Holland 0 Scotland 0

Holland 2 *(Jordi 66, Bergkamp 79)* Switzerland 0

England 2 *(Shearer 52, Gascoigne 79)* Scotland 0

Scotland 1 *(McCoist 36)* Switzerland 0

England 4 *(Shearer 23 pen, 57, Sheringham 51, 62)*
Holland 1 *(Kluivert 78)*

	P	W	D	L	F	A	Pts
England	3	2	1	0	7	2	7
Holland	3	1	1	1	3	4	4
Scotland	3	1	1	1	1	2	4
Switzerland	3	0	1	2	1	4	1

GROUP B

Spain 1 *(Alfonso 74)* Bulgaria 1 *(Stoichkov 65 pen)*

France 1 *(Dugarry 25)* Romania 0

Bulgaria 1 *(Stoichkov 3)* Romania 0

France 1 *(Djorkaeff 48)* Spain 1 *(Caminero 85)*

France 3 *(Blanc 20, Penev og 62, Loko 90)*
Bulgaria 1 *(Stoichkov 68)*

Spain 2 *(Manjarin 11, Amor 84)* Romania 1 *(Raducioiu 29)*

	P	W	D	L	F	A	Pts
France	3	2	1	0	5	2	7
Spain	3	1	2	0	4	3	5
Bulgaria	3	1	1	1	3	4	4
Romania	3	0	0	3	1	4	0

GROUP C

Germany 2 *(Ziege 26, Moller 32)* Czech Republic 0

Italy 2 *(Casiraghi 5, 52)* Russia 1 *(Tsimbalar 20)*

Czech Rep 2 *(Nedved 5, Bejbl 36)* Italy 1 *(Chiesa 18)*

Germany 3 *(Sammer 56, Klinsmann 77, 90)* Russia 0

Italy 0 Germany 0

Czech Rep 3 *(Suchoparek 7, Kuka 19, Smicer 89)*
Russia 3 *(Mostovoi 49, Tetradze 54, Beschastnikh 85)*

	P	W	D	L	F	A	Pts
Germany	3	2	1	0	5	0	7
Czech Republic	3	1	1	1	5	6	4
Italy	3	1	1	1	3	3	4
Russia	3	0	1	2	4	8	1

GROUP D

Denmark 1 *(B. Laudrup 22)* Portugal 1 *(Sa Pinto 53)*

Croatia 1 *(Vlaovic 85)* Turkey 0

Portugal 1 *(Fernando Couto 66)* Turkey 0

Croatia 3 *(Suker 53 pen, 89, Boban 80)* Denmark 0

Portugal 3 *(Figo 4, Joao Pinto 33, Domingos 83)* Croatia 0

Denmark 3 *(B. Laudrup 50 84, A. Nielsen 69)* Turkey 0

	P	W	D	L	F	A	Pts
Portugal	3	2	1	0	5	1	7
Croatia	3	2	0	1	4	3	6
Denmark	3	1	1	1	4	4	4
Turkey	3	0	0	3	0	5	0

QUARTER-FINALS

England 0 Spain 0 England 4–2 on pens, after extra time

France 0 Holland 0 France 5–4 on pens, after extra time

Germany 2 *(Klinsmann 21 pen, Sammer 59)* Croatia 1 *(Suker 51)*

Czech Republic 1 *(Poborsky 53)* Portugal 0

SEMI-FINALS

Czech Republic 0 France 0
Czech Republic 6–5 on pens, after extra time

Germany 1 *(Kuntz 16)* England 1 *(Shearer 3)*
Germany 6–5 on pens, after extra time

FINAL, 30 June, Wembley, London
Germany 2 *(Bierhoff 73, 94)* Czech Republic 1 *(Berger 58 pen)*
Germany, golden goal in extra time
HALF-TIME: 0–0 • 90 MINUTES: 1–1 • ATT: 76,000 • REF: Pairetto (Italy)
Germany: *Kopke, Babbel, Sammer, Helmer, Strunz, Hässler, Eilts (Bode 46), Scholl (Bierhoff 69), Ziege, Klinsmann, Kuntz.*
Czech Republic: *Kouba, Hornak, Rada, Kadlec, Suchoparek, Poborsky (Smicer 88), Nedved, Bejbl, Berger, Nemec, Kuka.*

The publishers would like to thank the following sources for their kind permission to reproduce the
pictures in this book:

Allsport U.K. Ltd./Shaun Botterill 3r, 7, 80b /Clive Brunskill 3l, 51, 67/Simon Bruty 76/Phil Cole 63/Michael Cooper 66/Nuno
Corriea 32, 62/Stu Forster 50, 58/Laurence Griffiths 52/Mike Hewitt 3c, 31, 70/Alex Livesey 26-7, 37/Jamie McDonald
20/Clive Mason 2/Tony O'Brien 56/Ben Radford 53/Mark Thompson 71

Corbis/Bettmann 74tl/Hulton-Deutsch Collection 73

EMPICS/Matthew Ashton 8, 23, 28, 46-7, 59, 61/Jon Buckle 65/Barry Coombs 22, 48-9/Mike Egerton 57/Tom Honan 24,
55/Ross Kinnaird 9/Tony Marshall 4-5, 34, 35, 42-3/John Marsh 19/Presse Sports 72/Peter Robinson 74br, 75/Neal Simpson
18, 39, 76b, 80t/Michael Steele 68

PA News/European Press Agency 10, 11, 12, 13, 21, 25, 30, 33, 36, 38, 40-1, 60, 64/Gabriel Bouys 54/David Kendall 29//Neil
Munns 45/Rebecca Naden 44, 69

Every effort has been made to acknowledge correctly and contact the source and/copyright holder
of each picture, and Carlton Books Limited apologises for any unintentional errors or omissions
which will be corrected in future editions of this book.